Living in Your Father's Embrace

A Revelation of <u>Your</u> Righteousness

Rudi Louw

Copyright © 2013 Rudi Louw Publishing

Revised edition, *"A Place Prepared for You"*

All rights reserved solely by the author. No part of this book may be reproduced in any form without the permission of the author.

Most Scripture quotations are taken from the RSV®, *Revised Standard Version*, Copyright © 1983 by Thomas Nelson, Inc.

Some Scripture quotations were taken from the NKJV, *New King James Version*, Copyright © 1983 by Thomas Nelson, Inc.

Some Scripture quotations are from the *New American Standard Bible,* Thomas Nelson Publishers. Copyright © 1960, 1963, 1968, 1971, 1973, 1975, 1977 by The Lockman Foundation.

All Scripture quotations not taken from the RSV, NKJV and NASV are a literal translation of the Scriptures and an effort to emphasize and clarify truth!

The Holy Scriptures are just that: HOLY. Statements enclosed in brackets were inserted into Scripture quotations to add emphasis or clarify the meaning of what is being said. The integrity of God's Word to Man was not compromised in any way. Due care and diligence was cautiously exercised to keep the Word of Truth intact.

Table of Contents

The Marvel of the Holy Bible 3

Acknowledgment 5

Prayer 15

1. *The Time of the Restoration of All Things HAS COME* 17

2. *Let Not Your Hearts Be Troubled* ...29

3. *In My Father's House Are Many Dwelling Places* 37

4. *The Way, The Truth, and The Life* . 59

5. *I Will Send the Helper to You* 79

6. *If You've Seen Me, You've Seen the Father* 97

7. *Righteousness: The Only Treasure Worth Pursuing* 105

8. *For With the Heart One Believes* . 131

About the Author 141

The Marvel of the Holy Bible

1. Uninterrupted Theme and Inspired Thought

It took *1,500 years* to compile the Holy Bible, involving *more than 40 different authors*. <u>Yet</u> the theme and inspired thought of Scripture, continues *uninterrupted* from author to author, from beginning till end.

2. Absence of Mythical Stories

Compare philosophies and theories about creation in the Middle East, Europe, Asia, Africa, and Latin America and you'll find mythical scenarios: gods feuding and cutting up other gods to form the heavens and the earth, etc.

In ancient Greek mythology, the Greeks see Atlas carrying the earth on his shoulders. In India, Hindus believe eight elephants carry the earth on their backs.

But in contrast, Job, the oldest book in the Holy Bible, declares that, *"God suspends the earth 'on nothing."(Job 26:7)*

This was said millennia before Isaac Newton discovered the invisible laws of gravity that delicately balance every planet and sun in its individual circuit.

Contrary to every other ancient attempt to give a creation account, *the Holy Bible pictures the creation of the earth in a very scientific manner.*

Example: In Genesis Chapter One, the continents are lifted from the seas then vegetation is formed and later animal life all reproducing *'according to its own kind'*, **thus recognizing the fixed genetic laws.** In addition, we have the bringing forth of man and woman, *all done by God in a dignified and proper manner, without mythological adornments.*

The balance or remainder of the Holy Bible follow suite.

The narratives are **true historical documents***, faithfully reflecting society and culture* **as history and archaeology would discover them thousands of years later. Not only is the Holy Bible historically accurate, it is also reliable when it deals with scientifically reliable subjects.**

It was never intended to be a textbook on history, science, mathematics, or medicine. *However, when its writers touch on these subjects,* **they often state facts that scientific advancement would not reveal, or even consider, until thousands of years later.**

While many have doubted the accuracy of the Holy Bible, time and continued research have consistently demonstrated that the Word of God is better informed than its critics.

3. Intactness

Of all the ancient works of substantial size, *the Holy Bible survives intact, against all odds and expectations.*

Compared with other ancient writings, the Holy Bible has more manuscripts as evidence to support it than any ten pieces of classical literature combined!

The plays of William Shakespeare, for instance, were written about four hundred years ago, after the invention of the printing press. Many of his original writings and words have been lost in numerous sections, *yet the Holy Bible's uncanny preservation, has weathered thousands of years of wars, contradictions, persecutions, fires and invasions.*

Through the centuries Jewish scribes have preserved the Holy Bible's Old Covenant text, **such as no other manuscripts has ever been preserved. They kept tabs on every letter, syllable, word and paragraph.** *They continued from generation to generation to appoint and train special groups of men within their culture,* **whose sole duty it was to preserve and transmit these documents, <u>with perfect accuracy and fidelity</u>.**

Who ever bothered to count the letters, syllables, or words of Plato, Aristotle, or Seneca for that matter?

When it comes to the New Testament, the actual number of preserved manuscripts is so great that it becomes overwhelming**.** ***There are more than 5,680 Greek manuscripts, more than 10,000 Latin Vulgate manuscripts and at least 9,300 other versions. Further still, there exists an additional 25,000 manuscript copies of portions of the New Testament.* No other document of antiquity even begins to approach such numbers.**

The closest in comparison is Homer's <u>Iliad</u>, with only 643 manuscripts. The first complete work of Homer only dates back to the 13th century.

4. Unmatched Accuracy in Predictive Foretelling

The Holy Bible is unmatched in accuracy in predictive foretelling. No other ancient work even begins to attempt this.

Other books, such as the Koran, the Book of Mormon, and parts of the Veda claim divine inspiration; ***but none of these books contain predictive foretelling.***

This one undeniable fact we know for certain: *While microscopic scrutiny would show up the imperfections, blemishes and defects of any work of man, <u>it magnifies the beauties and perfection of God</u>. Just as every flower displays in accurate detail the reflection and perfection of beauty, <u>so does the Word of Truth when it is scrutinized</u>.*

Historian Philip Schaff wrote:

"Without money and weapons, Jesus the Christ conquered more millions, than Alexander, Caesar, Mohammed, and Napoleon. Without science and learning, He (Jesus the Christ) shed more light on things human and divine than all philosophers and scholars combined. Without the eloquence of schools, He (Jesus the Christ) spoke such words of life as was never spoken before or since and produced effects which lie beyond the reach of orator or poet. Without writing a single line, He (Jesus the Christ) set more pens in motion and furnished themes for more sermons, orations, discussions, learned

volumes, works of art, and songs of praise **than the whole army of great men of ancient and modern times combined.**" (*The Person of Christ*, p33. 1913)

Today, there are literally billions of Bibles in more than 2,000 languages.

Isn't it about time you find out what it really has to say?

Hey listen, the Holy Bible is all about Jesus, the Messiah, the Christ...

...and everything about Jesus Christ is really about YOU!!

Study Tips:

Read 2 Corinthians 5:14, 16, 18, 19, and 21.

In the light of these Scriptures, it should be obvious that, if you want to study the Holy Bible, *you should study it in the light of mankind's redemption!*

Feed daily on redemption realities found in the book of Acts, in Romans Chapters One through Eight, and in Ephesians, Colossians, and Galatians, also in 1 Peter Chapter One, 2 Peter Chapter One, James Chapter 1, as well as in 1 and 2 Corinthians.

Acknowledgment

I want to acknowledge and thank one of my mentors in the faith, Francois du Toit, for blessing and impacting my life with revelation knowledge.

The portion on *"The Marvel of the Holy Bible"* was borrowed from his website, http://www.MirrorWord.net/ as students so often feel they have a right to do with things that come from teachers they respect. Just as Galatians 6:6 says, *"Let him who is taught the Word **share in all good things** with him who teaches."*

To all our many dear friends and our precious family whom we love, and to Chase Aderhold and all those who helped me with this project:

Especially to my sweet wife Carmen, for all the love and support,

THANK YOU!

I love and appreciate you so very much.

"Eye has not seen,
nor ear heard,

Nor have entered
into the heart of man

The things
which God has prepared
for those who love Him.

But God has revealed them to us
through His Spirit.

For the spirit searches all things,
yes, even the deep things of God.
Now we have received,

*not the spirit of the world,
but the Spirit who is from God,*

*that we might know
the things*

*that have been freely
given to us by God"*

- 1Corinthians 1:9-12

Prayer

Father, the Scriptures declare that, "*The path of the righteous is like the light of the morning, ever increasing in intensity until the sun in all its splendor rules the day."*

Thank you for Your precious, anointed Word testified to in the Scriptures.

Thank you, Father, that You have revealed Your heart in Your Word made flesh, Jesus the Christ.

Father, I thank you that You, by Your Holy Spirit, will give to those who read this book a spirit of wisdom and revelation into Your knowledge;

…that the eyes of their understanding will be opened, and that they will **know** *what You have called them into*, and how rich and glorious *Your inheritance* **in them** is.

I thank you for those who comprehend the revelation in this book, that Christ, *in His fullness,* will from now on **dwell** *in their hearts through faith*;

…that they will indeed be rooted and grounded *in Your love*,

…and *fully* comprehend the width, length, depth, and height of it – *to **intimately know** the love of Christ,* which surpasses knowledge;

…*and so be* **filled** *with* **all the fullness** *of God.*

Father I also thank you that *in the grasping and laying a hold of these things;*

…***their love*** will increase even more and more;

…*through Your knowledge;*

…and all discernment into *Your truth of redemption*;

…so they may approve the things that are excellent,;

…and that they may be sincere and *without offense all their life long.*

I thank you that, through the revelation in this book *getting into people's hearts and consciousness*,

…they will all be gloriously *filled with all the fruits of righteousness;*

…*through Christ Jesus* **dwelling** *in them by the Spirit of Truth*;

…to Your glory and praise forever Father God.

Amen

Chapter 1

The Time of the Restoration of All Things HAS COME

I want to start off by thanking you for taking the time to read this book. This book was not written to be read in a casual way, as one would a novel. It contains revelation into some things you may or may not have heard or considered before.

Open yourself up to study the revelation contained in this book and be like the people of Berea the apostle Paul ministered to in Acts 17:11. Read this book with a desire and anticipation to not only gain knowledge, but to hear from God your Father.

It contains within it the voice and call of Father God to every human being on the face of this earth. If you take heed to it and comprehend it, I guarantee it will change your life!

Let us begin by taking a look at Acts 3:19-21,

19 *"Repent therefore and be converted, that your sins may be blotted out,* ***so that times of refreshing may come from the presence of the Lord****,*

20 *and that He may send Jesus Christ, who was preached to you before,*

21 *whom Heaven must receive **until the times of restoration of all things**, which God has spoken of by the mouth of all His holy prophets since the world began."*

- Acts 3:19-21 (NKJV)

19 *"Repent therefore and **return**, that your sins may be wiped away**, in order that times of refreshing may come from the presence of the Lord**;*

20 *and that He may send Jesus, **the Christ appointed for you**,*

21 *whom Heaven must receive **until the period of restoration of all things** about which God spoke by the mouth of His holy prophets, from ancient time."*

- Acts 3:19-21 (NASV)

This scripture lays a firm foundation for what I want to say. Peter says about the apostle Paul that *he writes about some things in his letters that are hard to grasp*, which some twist to their own ruin as they so often do also the rest of the Scriptures.

You may not find my writings any different from that of the apostle Paul's unless I first get into this passage of Scripture and explain some things.

Reading what the apostle Peter had to say to these people, it may sound like the Scriptures are trying to say that Heaven received Jesus and He's up there right now, *and we are just going to have to hold on until He comes back again.* But if you read it carefully, you will come to realize that Peter is not speaking about some future event. Peter is speaking about the fact that ***now*** *refreshing may come from the presence of the Lord!* As you read this text again, you might also realize,

"…the times of restoration of all things, which God has spoken by the mouth of all His holy prophets since the world began **has come.**"

"The time of the restoration of all things **has come**..."

Notice what Peter says here in Acts 19:21,

"...Heaven received Jesus until the times of restoration of all things."

Nothing God spoke about through the prophets remain unfulfilled. *Every single thing God has spoken about through the prophets* **concerning the incarnation of Christ and His work of redemption, have all been fulfilled**.

My Bible says in Galatians 4:4 that ***the fullness of time has come.*** ***The time period between the incarnation and the ascension of Jesus is what is being referred to as*** *the fullness of time*. ***The times of restoration of all these things*** *have come about* ***in Christ's incarnation and His work of redemption.***

That is what the work of redemption is all about. *Jesus' death, burial, and resurrection* ***brought about the restoration of all things.***

Acts 3:24 confirms this, by saying that all the prophets foretold *"**these days**"*.

And so does 1 Peter 1:10-12,

10 *"**Of this salvation** the prophets have inquired and searched diligently, who prophesied **of the grace that would come to YOU,***

11 *searching what, and what manner of time the Spirit of Christ who was in them was indicating when* He testified beforehand of the sufferings of Christ ***and the glories that would follow.***

12 *To them it was revealed that, not to themselves, but* to US *they were ministering the things* which now have been reported to you *through those who have preached the gospel to you by the Holy Spirit sent from Heaven – things which angels desire to look into."*

Do not get mad at me now, for I do not mean to offend you, but I do believe that *way too many well-meaning people get so easily preoccupied with so-called prophetic words concerning the future that they develop the wrong emphasis.*

Some people can supposedly tell you all about the end times **but still have no clue about what happened in the fullness of time.** They still have no clue about **what God has to say to us in the incarnation and in redemption, or in the life, death, burial, resurrection, and ascension of His Son**.

Many sincere, but ignorant people **have lost their focus** on what **genuinely matters.** I do not say this to shame them, but they have been *led astray from the simplicity that is in Christ Jesus.* **Instead of focusing on the gospel (on what God has to say to us in the incarnation and work of redemption), they are way too caught up in the so-called signs of the times.**

Hebrews 1:1,

"**God, who at various times and in different ways spoke** (in fragments of thought and incomplete prophetic pictures) **in time past to the fathers by the prophets, has in these last days spoken** (in totality and clarity) **to us, in and by His Son.**"

The one big event which God, through the prophets foretold, the one event they focused upon, *the event they most prophesied about **was the fullness of time: The incarnation and work of redemption. God's whole <u>focus</u> is not on the future, but on the incarnation of Christ and what His death brought about for all mankind.***

Through the holy prophets of old, God foretold "***<u>these days</u>***" *more than any other days,* ***revealing to us His emphasis.*** He had more to say about "***<u>these days</u>***" than any other days: **past, present or future**.

So then, looking at those Scriptures in Acts Chapter 3:19-21, ***we are not speaking of a time that has not fully come yet.*** Jesus the Christ was received up to Heaven. He remained in Heaven throughout the time of the fulfillment of the prophecies. He remained in Heaven until all was fulfilled in His death and resurrection and the time fully came for Heaven to release the Son of God *in order for times of refreshing to come to us <u>now</u>, from the very presence of the Lord.*

*"The times of **restoration** of <u>all things</u>..."*

I believe God wants to **restore** "<u>*all things*</u>"...**all things!**

*In the coming of Jesus Christ and His successful work of redemption, God brought man, **here on planet earth**, back into a **restored** relationship with Himself.*

The word *"restoration"* used in Acts 3:21 means, as indicated in the original Greek language *'TO REINSTATE SOMETHING TO ITS EXACT RIGHTFUL STATE OF GLORY.'*

The most important of the *"all things"* we lost through Adam is **righteousness**.

God wants to restore everything Adam lost through the fall, through sin.

In Christ Jesus, God intends to **restore** it **_ALL_** starting with the most crucial thing: **RIGHTEOUSNESS!**

God wants to restore righteousness *the way He had it in mind in the first place.* When God first brought man forth out of Himself, He had in mind *a person with whom he could fully relate.* A relationship where there would be *transparency.* A relationship where there would be *no sense of separation, no sense of guilt, no sense of fear, no sense of inferiority, no complex, no negative vibe, but* **equality**.

That's what God wants, **nothing less!**

That is exactly why God wants to **blot out** sin! He doesn't want to just kind of deal with it and paralyze it a little bit, or give you a tranquilizer drug from time to time so you can keep sin subdued for a little while at least, and feel a little better. Then, all of a sudden, the drug wears off and sin resurrects again, bringing you under its dominion.

This is exactly what life was like under the Old Covenant. People could bring a little blood sacrifice and, only for a moment, there would be a release of that guilt, that pressure. They would feel a little better and they would feel right. *But* it would only last for a short period of time, because they would inevitably fall and stumble again, *having been given another occasion to sin through the law.* Sin would indeed revive and become a powerful thing again, undoing the release they experienced through the blood sacrifice.

Sin represents that whole thing that held man guilty before God. God wants to *completely deal with it, to do away with it*. He wants to *blot it out*. He wants to *wipe it out*, root and all. He wants to uproot that whole thing *from your way of thinking.*

He wants to get it out of your system *so that you can be restored in righteousness,* **as God originally had it in mind,** because from the position of being restored in that original righteousness, you can then begin to understand and appreciate **and operate** *in spirit dominion!*

Operating in spirit dominion means you are walking in a place of having authority over all the enemy's power. It means you are *repossessing* what the thief took from God's kids (mankind).

Operating in spirit dominion means *you can stand* against the devil *and he will flee from you.* It means you can *take his spoil*, you can *release* the prey from his clutches. It means *receiving* the restoration of *"all things"*.

That is what God wants for His kids. God wants for us as His partners, as His co-rulers, to *operate* in spirit dominion. He wants us to go forth and witness the darkness *flee before us* because of the *dominion* of the Spirit of God *released in our hearts.*

Friend, please listen to me, *it is absolutely, vitally necessary for us to understand* **our righteousness.** **We are profoundly mistaken if we think we can *truly walk* in that dominion of the Spirit before we *fully understand and walk in our righteousness,*** *the way God sees it, and declares it to be, the way God wants us to understand it and believe it and enjoy walking in that righteousness!*

Until we fully understand *and enter into* our righteousness, we can forget about being the ones *to see the actual restoration* of *"all things"* in our generation.

I'm telling you, if there is one thing the devil would seek to keep you ignorant in, it's in the area of righteousness.

Why?

Because he knows that if he can tamper with your mind, with your thinking, with your righteousness-consciousness, and bring you into sin-consciousness *where you are ruled by your emotions, and you feel guilty all the time, and you feel inferior all the time,* **then you become a zero threat to his kingdom.** Then you can even go through the motions and do all the right things *and still be defeated*, just like those guys we read about in the book of Acts who went to try to cast out devils in the name of the Jesus whom Paul preached.

Those devils jumped on them and almost tore them apart. The devils said to them, *'Hey man, we know Jesus, we have heard of this man Paul, but who are you?!'*

In other words, *'We can smell your lack of total conviction a mile away. You are not even convinced of these things yourself, you don't know who you really are. And your lack of confidence betrays you. You are weak in faith, so who do you think you are to come and try and cast us out?! We only listen to people who* **know** *their authority, who* **believe** *and* **walk in** *their righteousness, the ones who* **actually** *walk with God and* **know** *God!'*

The devils used those people's own *ignorance, double-mindedness, and lack of confidence before God, their weak and inaccurate, incomplete faith,* against them to defeat them.

That's why I'm saying that we are profoundly mistaken if we think we can walk in victory ourselves, *let alone launch out in ministering to others,* before we thoroughly understand and can say, '***I know God's reality. I know reality itself, from God's perspective, I know the legal grounds for my righteousness. I truly do know the legal implications upon which my righteousness is established.***'

You see, as God begins to release to our understanding **what reality looks like**, I mean, as God begins to release to our understanding the legal foundation for, the legal grounds to, our righteousness, *He gives us the opportunity to enjoy our righteousness* **practically, in our experience.**

Chapter 2

Let Not Your Hearts Be Troubled

Now that we have established that *the fullness of time* **has come**, that *the restoration of all things* **came about in Jesus Christ** and that *our righteousness is thus* **at hand, within our reach**, let us take a look at John 14 where Jesus is talking to His disciples. He was speaking about *what He was about to accomplish in His death, burial, resurrection and ascension.*

This is one of the last recorded conversations that Jesus had with His disciples while He was still in the flesh, before the crucifixion.

1 *"Let not your hearts be troubled; believe in God, believe also in Me.*

2 *In My Father's house are many dwelling places (rooms, abodes, mansions); if it were not so, I would have told you; for* **I go to prepare a place for you**.

3 *And if I go* **and prepare a place <u>for you</u>**, *I will come again, and receive you to Myself;*

that where I am, there you may be also." - John 14:1-3 (NASV)

In reading this passage, it is essential for us to understand what the disciples were going through before we can actually understand what is taking place here, and how valuable what Jesus was sharing with them really is, to them, *as well as to us*.

The disciples, through their relationship with Jesus, came into a relationship with God that, up to that point in man's history, *had not been universally man's privilege to enjoy since the fall. It had not been accessible to the vast majority since the fall of Adam.* **But now,** through the disciple's relationship with Jesus, they began to relate to the Almighty God in a way that they'd never related to Him before, because it wasn't possible to them, *due to the dominion of ingrained ignorance and darkness since the Fall.* But Jesus began to give them a glimpse of what was about to become available to all men everywhere after His death: *the privilege of freely being able to relate to God.*

Jesus began to afford them, in their relationship with Him, a new relationship with God. *He began to introduce to them the whole concept of God being their Father.*

In the Old Covenant portion of the Scriptures, you don't read about that, because **The Law emphasized separation. It *created even*** *more distance.* **Because of its focus on sin, and man's efforts and self-righteous, fleshly pride,** *it further condemned man.*

And in the light of that condemnation and guilt, and wrath, and judgment, and feelings of God being so holy and focused on sin, therefore being inapproachable **...and feelings of 'I am so unworthy and worthless and unwelcome before God' …it distorted the real image and likeness of God and created the somewhat misguided concept that the Great God over everything is out there, and you just better make sure you step in line or else His wrath is going to fall on you.**

John 1:17,

"For the Law was given through Moses;"

(secondhand, indirect, *with distance and separation built into it from the start*),

*"**BUT** grace and **TRUTH CAME;**"*

(first hand, in person, up close and personal)

"…through (or in) *Jesus Christ."*

Jesus came and began to give man the opportunity to relate to God again as *'Abba Father'* **or** *'Daddy'.*

He, being the expressed image and likeness of God, *began to restore again the concept that*

Creator God had companionship in mind when He brought man forth out of Himself and created a body for us to live in here on planet earth.

God didn't have in mind a bunch of robots, which would just serve Him in some religious way. He wanted to, and was about to, through His Son, *restore man to his original sonship.*

Galatians 4:4-5,

4 *"But <u>when the fullness of time **had come**</u>, God sent forth His Son, born of a woman, born under the law,*

5 *to **redeem** those who were under the law, **that we might receive** <u>the adoption as **sons**</u>."*

This term *"**adoption**"* is not like our modern concept of adoption. *It is not simply a putting into the family; taking a stranger's kid and putting them into your family.* This term *"**adoption**"* used is actually an old world concept. It has to do with *an establishing of the legal position of a son that vitally affects the son's life.* Adoption is a term that speaks of the *elevation* of sons, who are coming of age, *into a special relationship with their dads, which was always meant for them,* wherein they experience equality and friendship with him as their father.

They are being brought into their rightful place as mature sons, for they are the legal heirs to their Father's estate. It is the privilege of *sons being brought into fullness, into full, intimate, close, personal friendship and relationship with their Father*. **The relationship is that of friendship, dignity, honor and intimacy, established upon full acceptance and embrace.** (Read Galatians 4:1-7)

You see, the Son of God became the son of man, *so that the sons of men might again enjoy being the sons of God.*

That's exactly what the Father had in mind when He sent His Son to come and rub shoulders with us here on planet earth.

Jesus was beginning to give to his disciples the opportunity to relate to God in a new way as "*Abba Father*," as *"Daddy"*. He began to introduce to them *the Father.* He began to give to them an opportunity to relate, intimately, to God, as THEIR *Father.*

They did not fully comprehend it at the time, but they began to sense it. They began to enter into a freedom with God *that they never had before under the law and under religion.*

Maybe now, in the light of this, we can more fully appreciate their reaction when Jesus began to speak to them about His coming death, and about the fact that He would again go to the Father.

They were *seriously disturbed* in their hearts because, within the revelation that began to unfold to them that they could relate to God *as Father,* they became dependent on Jesus.

Being still under the whole system of the law and sin, their religious concepts restricted them. They could not indirectly relate to God *as Father.* Yet they related to Him through Jesus. Jesus was their direct link to God. Without Him *they felt that they would stand to lose all that they had gained.*

And now Jesus was speaking to them and bringing their worst fears to life by saying that He would die and go back to His Father.

Just the mere thought of the finality of this immediately made them feel threatened. Their reaction was, *'Jesus, please don't walk out on us now …we cannot afford to see you go away from us, Jesus.'*

They felt threatened by the idea that Jesus would be crucified, depart, and go away from them forever. Fear and trouble was ruling in their hearts. They were looking at the whole situation *from a natural human point of view, from an emotional, soulish point of view.* That's why they were troubled in their hearts.

It was then that Jesus said,

"Let not your hearts be troubled." - John 14:1

God doesn't want troubled hearts **because troubled hearts cannot enjoy righteousness**. Jesus challenged them, *"Believe in God, believe also in Me."*

In today's terms, He said something like, *'Hey man, do not fear! **Believe!**'*

*'<u>Trust</u> in the goodness of God, and <u>trust</u> also in Me. **Believe** what I say …and **believe** God that in whatever He has planned and is busy with, **He has you in mind!**'*

By saying this He was trying to prepare the environment for them to receive what He was about to say to them. He was trying to inform them of what He was about to accomplish on their behalf, *but He also knew there was no way they could receive anything while there was a negative environment in their hearts, while trouble reigned in their spirits.*

In spite of Jesus' efforts, they still felt troubled and anxious, *and they began to resent Jesus.*

I can just imagine their thoughts:

'Jesus, you brought us into something so unique, something so precious, and now you begin to speak of going away and leaving us out here by ourselves.'

'We don't have a handle on these precious things for ourselves yet!'

If they were only listening, Jesus' words could have helped them.

He said to them,

"**BELIEVE (Trust)!** *Believe in God, believe also in Me..."*

"(Trust) in God, (trust) also in Me. Come on now, **get your faith to operate again, BELIEVE (Trust!),** *Amen?!"*

- John 14:1

Believe is the verb of faith; **it's the action of faith.** And so, **because of what your faith knows to be true, therefore to believe (or trust)**, is a decision we make in the face of trouble.

While we look at anything from a human point of view, *from an emotional, soulish point of view,* fear will dominate, **and we will be unable to operate in spirit dominion.**

Faith on the other hand, immediately deals with anxiety. When faith is quickened and we make a decision to operate in faith, <u>fear is dispelled</u>.

Chapter 3

In My Father's House Are Many Dwelling Places

All right, now Jesus begins to bring them to this revelation that I also want to share with you. It is the main reason for this book:

"In My Father's house are many dwelling places (rooms, abodes, mansions), *if it were not so, I would have told you; for I go to prepare a place for you."*

- John 14:2 (NASV)

He was addressing their anxieties, trying to calm their hearts. But more than that, He was trying to get their attention. What He was about to share with them was so momentous they couldn't afford to miss it. He was eager to tell them what was about to happen, ***for it would alter our reality here on earth forever!***

This is what He said, in common English:

'I'm going to My Father, but don't close your ears now, hang in there with Me. Trust Me, and believe the things I'm saying: ***where I'm***

going there's room for you. *If it were not so, I wouldn't have led you on, I would have told you so from the beginning.'*

The words '**ROOM**' and '**PLACE**' in the original language are translated from the word '**MENO**', which comes from the words *'ABIDE <u>WITH</u>, TO CONTINUE <u>WITH</u>, TO DWELL TOGETHER <u>WITH</u>'.*

It is the same word used in the next chapter, Chapter 15, where we read about the relationship between a branch and the vine:

*"**Abide** in Me,"*

…and *"Let My words **abide** in you."*

It speaks of <u>an abiding place</u>.

You see, we with our Sunday-school mentality of *"mansions"* as in the King James translation of that word, have in mind all kinds of beautiful, elegant buildings in Heaven, out there in outer space somewhere. It is easy to start building all these marvelous imaginations about our *"mansions"* having at least four bedrooms and a thick carpet in the bedroom, with an indoor swimming pool and so on, and so on. Because of ignorance, even still today, people develop all these ideas about some mansion that Jesus is building for them out in outer space somewhere in some weird, unknown place called Heaven.

If we carefully read these scriptures, we will discover that *it is certainly not* the kind of thought process Jesus had in mind for us to develop when He said those words. **He was speaking of a restored relationship, not literal mansions. In the face of His death, He was prophesying and speaking of the things that would soon come about by His accomplishment on that cross *for us*.** He said, *"I go to prepare **a place FOR YOU**."*

If we study the implications of the fall and sin then we can easily see how sin came as a thief to rob us of *our place in God*. We were robbed *from enjoying the presence of God.* We were left with a sense of guilt, condemnation, and inferiority, and we were outside of what we were designed and brought forth to be inside of. *We were outside of fellowship with God. We could no longer relate to Him intimately.*

Isaiah 59:1 & 2 says that,

"Your sins became as a wall that separated you from God."

But now Jesus says in John 14:1,

*"I go to prepare a place **for you**."*

Jesus is at the right hand of His Father right now, occupying the office of Mediator of the New Covenant. He, in His very person, in His very being, is God, and man, united in one body. He represents us in Heaven.

There is a man seated at the right hand of God. He is there right now as surety of the New Covenant, and to be the enforcing agent of our inheritance. That's what He is doing up there. That is His job description right now. He is not building mansions, He's not in the mansion building business right now, He is not a building contractor up in Heaven.

He prepared that place He is talking about in the three days and nights when He suffered in the flesh, *for us.*

It was when He became sin, <u>on **OUR** behalf</u>, that He prepared *a place* **for US**.

It was when He faced sin's judgment, it was when He became sin and stood before the throne of Justice, that He prepared *a place* **for YOU and for ME**. That's the whole purpose of the New Covenant.

We can get so carried away about the mansions in the sky that we fail to comprehend and understand what Jesus actually said and did.

The truth is, *"He* (God the Father) *made Him* (Jesus) *who knew no sin, to be sin **<u>for US</u>**, so that **WE might become** the righteousness of God **in Him** (there in His work of redemption)."*

– 2 Corinthians 5:21

2 Corinthians 5:16 says,

16 *"Once, we regarded Christ from a natural, human point of view, but we regard Him thus no longer!"*

Now we regard Him as representing all mankind's freedom, we regard Him as Savior of the world!

I want to tell you that once this revelation begins to burn within your heart, it becomes more precious to you than the fanciest mansion you ever dreamed up.

Why?

Because *through this revelation, you and I have access into the most complete, most fulfilling relationship that man can ever enjoy.* You see, it doesn't matter then whether a man lives under a thatched roof, a tin roof, a grass roof on a mud hut, a copper dome, or no roof at all. ***It can no longer add or take away from his life.***

Let's get back to John 14:3,

*"...I go and prepare <u>a place</u> **for you**. Then I will come again and receive you to Myself; that where I am, **there you may be also**."*

Now we used to think that that little word "*Then*" used here was referring to the mysterious event talked about by Paul in 1 Corinthians 15:51-53.

But John 14:19-20 says:

19 *"A little while longer <u>and the world will see Me no more, **but you will see Me**</u>.*

*Because I live, you will **live** also."*

20 *At that day, you will know that I am **in** My Father, and you **in** Me, and I **in** you."*

The point I want to make here is that, if Jesus had that event in mind which Paul was talking about in 1 Corinthians 15:51-53, He wouldn't have said:

*"…you will see Me, **but the world wouldn't.**"*

Because in that event Paul talked about, *the veil between spirit dimension and natural dimension would suddenly be removed* and Jesus, along with all the hosts of heaven, *would suddenly appear* **and eternal REALITY would suddenly be upon us all** *and every eye would see Him*.

But now in this 19th verse of John Chapter 14 Jesus says that,

*"…only the **believers** will be able to <u>see</u> Him."*

He was speaking about our interaction with the Spirit of Truth. *Revelation knowledge* **is**

what He was talking about, because revelation knowledge, *insight and understanding, knowing the truth about Him, and about what He came to accomplish FOR US, BELIEVING THESE THINGS is the only access that an individual has.*

<u>That faith</u> is our only way to be born anew, brought back into fellowship with God, to come back into righteousness. *It's the only way to come back into a position of being able to relate to the Creator God* ***without a sense of guilt, without a sense of shame or inferiority, but with a perfect, perfect sense of confidence; <u>standing fulfilled and whole in the presence of God</u>.***

John 14:3,

*"…**that where I am, <u>there you may be also.</u>***"

This is what Jesus has in mind. He says,

'Let not your hearts be troubled, believe in Me, come on now, ***believe*** *in Me.* ***Change your minds.*** *Trust in Me!* ***Don't listen to those fears or those lies in your mind.*** *Don't look at Me from an emotional, soulish point of view, or from a natural, mere human point of view!'*

'This is what I have in mind:'

'I'm going to prepare <u>a place for YOU</u>.'

'I'm not going to leave you comfortless and helpless. I'm not going to leave you desolate. I'm not going to leave you like orphans. Everything I am about to do is for YOU!'

He says in Verse 18,

"I will come to you;

…to receive you to Myself;

*…so that **YOU** may be where I am **also**."*

But where are you Jesus? Where are you?

I want us to first of all see this: *Before we can appreciate our righteousness, we need to understand His righteousness.*

Before we can fully understand 2 Corinthians 5:21, *"He* (God the Father) *made Him* (Jesus) *who knew no sin, Sin on our behalf **that we might become His righteousness**,"* **we must first understand His righteousness. We must first understand what His righteousness is all about.**

What is the righteousness of Jesus Christ? Do you think that Jesus *feels all embarrassed* in His Father's presence? Do you think that Jesus *needs to wear certain kinds of masks or put on some facade* to somehow *try and promote Himself* in His Father's presence? Do you think that Jesus *needs to come with all kinds of nervous 'small talk' or nice sounding little religious clichés* when He approaches His Father?

No, He doesn't!

Can you just picture Jesus in His Father's presence? Just imagine with me ***the love Jesus enjoys.*** Imagine *the kind of **openness**, the kind of **trust** and **transparency*** between them. Can you imagine *the sense of blamelessness, innocence, and companionship Jesus enjoys?*

Now, can you dare imagine *ALL THAT* <u>belonging to YOU</u>?

Two individuals that *enjoy that kind of relationship* can sometimes *just sit in silence and look and stare at and admire each other without a word.* They don't even need to *say* anything.

I dare say most people, *when it comes to a relationship with Father God,* live so far from that. Somehow believers think that when they approach the presence of God they need to pray a certain way, they need to say things just in a certain religious kind of way, with pleasant sounding little religious clichés, or they need to sing nice sounding religious songs full of almost meaningless, nice sounding, religious words, even though they don't even know what half those words actually mean *because, somehow, that will now really bring the manifest presence of God into their midst!*

Listen, **God is interested in *your inner man, your spirit man, <u>engaged</u> in His TRUTH.*** That's where true worship originates from. God looks *at the heart.* There is no formula, no religious format that can substitute that. God is looking for **adoration <u>from the heart</u>.** God is looking *for* **faith.**

He just wants us to come into His presence *with confidence.* If you will dare to do this, to come this way, *through embracing and applying the TRUTH, coming into His presence with a new, deep faith confidence,* you will see how *God is going to release you* **to relate to Him, to touch His presence!**

Through this revelation of, *'I am* **actually** *made righteous through Jesus' work of redemption,'* God is going to *allow you to stand and to handle and* **to experience His presence.**

As we learn to relate to His intimate presence, we will begin to see more of the manifestations of the glory of God, more of the love and the presence and the power of God in our corporate meetings because we've come to <u>know</u> Him in the privacy of our own hearts first!

In our private times with Him, *we learn when to* speak, and sing, and prophesy. But we also learn *how to just be quiet* in His presence, *just* **communicating from the heart with Him,** *just communicating* **from our hearts to His.**

God wants to bring us to a place *where He may freely communicate,* where He may *demonstrate and manifest, in us* and *to us* and *through us,* **what is in His Word, what is *in His thoughts* and *in His heart!***

Before we can come to that place, we need to understand and fully grasp **this place Jesus brought US into.** ***A place equal to His own, a place of righteousness, a place of intimate friendship and companionship.***

Jesus *enjoys* that place 24 hours a day, and there are no hours in His day, because He is *eternal, He enjoys eternal **life,*** **Hallelujah!**

He **is** righteous before God, legally *and vitally.* Jesus is **as righteous as <u>can be</u>** in His Father's presence. ***And He went and prepared that exact same place <u>for US</u>.***

I pray that ***you can see*** with me ***the implications*** of this revelation:

"…where I am, THERE <u>YOU</u> may be ALSO."

It is by far the greatest revelation you can receive in the whole Bible! ***Where Jesus is, you and I may be also.***

<u>**YOU**</u> ***may be* where Jesus *is!***

You may partake of a restored relationship with God to such a degree that it's not

secondhand, it's not just reconditioned. It's brand new and beautiful and rich.

1 Corinthians 1:9,

*"God is faithful who has **called us into <u>the fellowship of</u> the Son**."*

He's called us into the exact same fellowship, the exact same quality! Nothing less than the same. *It's the same, the exact same quality of open, intimate, up close and personal, transparent friendship and fellowship* with the eternal God. And *it's available to man*, even wretched, sinful, pitiable man. *But we are no longer that. I understand I am a new creature, created in Christ Jesus, in His work of redemption unto love and unto good works, created there in Him,* **after the exact image** *of my Creator!*

I understand it, I grasp it, <u>and I believe it</u>! And it's mine!

*"Once we were ...**but now we are.**"*

    - 1 Corinthians 6:11, and Ephesians 5:8.

It is absolutely imperative for every believer to study these truths ***until it <u>rules</u> in your spirit.***

The Spirit of God, through the Word of Truth, will bring into your mind *the ability to comprehend these things.* With your mind on natural things you cannot comprehend these things. *They are far above ...they are spiritually discerned.* **But with your mind set on actually understanding these things, <u>you are well able to comprehend them</u>** *and appreciate them and appropriate them.*

You were custom designed for these things. Custom designed *to know them, and enjoy them and live them!*

God, by His Spirit, will bring you into these things through an understanding of righteousness, through revelation knowledge, because you cannot enter into these things if you do not understand righteousness, **if you do not understand** *what happened on that cross and in that resurrection and ascension* **ON YOUR BEHALF.**

The moment the revelation of YOUR righteousness comes into your heart, the Bible opens up to you. You begin to see it *like you have never seen it before*. *Oh, you can't stop reading it, you want to consume it, you want to eat it, you want to drink it, you want to breathe it, you want to speak it, you want to live it… because you are **addicted** to it!*

Why?

Because the understanding of YOUR righteousness *is the only key that will unlock* **the storehouse of God's treasure** *to your spirit!*

I am trying my best in this book to help you receive revelation *as far as **YOUR righteousness** is concerned and **the treasure of it!***

If the revelation *that these things are fully yours NOW* doesn't come immediately, don't panic, *just take the seed.* Just take the words in this book and these Scriptures I am quoting to you *and go read it again and keep it in your heart, think upon it there.*

You might have to read portions of this book more than once *until the revelation of YOUR righteousness gets down on the inside of you* because it is vitally essential that you *understand **what it actually means** to be **righteous** before God so you can treasure it!*

The apostle Peter exhorts us in 2 Peter 1:19,

"We also have the prophetic word made more sure (because it was fulfilled)*, **which you do well to heed**, as a light that shines in a dark place, <u>UNTIL the day dawns</u>* (until the light comes on; **until a full understanding comes**) *and the morning star* (the full revelation; clarity of insight and understanding) *rises in your hearts."*

If there is one thing the devil would desire for your life, it would be for you *to remain ignorant concerning YOUR righteousness.*

The longer the devil can keep you ignorant, *the more he can dominate you with his lies* and get away with things he shouldn't be able to get away with *in **your** life.*

I hope this makes you fighting mad, to the point where you make a decision *to do whatever it takes to no longer be ignorant concerning YOUR righteousness.*

I have counseled people who had problems with smoking, drinking, and all kinds of other persistent, destructive, negative habits. Some of them told me how they've had devils of smoking and devils of drinking cast out of them, and all kinds of other devils cast out of them and how they have gone through all kinds of inner-healing classes, as well as this method and that one, and yet at the end of it all *they were no freer than they were before. In fact some of them got worse,* **still trapped in a spiral of bondage, without finding freedom.**

But as I simply began to share with them the revelation of THEIR righteousness, *you could just see the shackles come off.* The minute the revelation of THEIR righteousness dawned on their hearts, suddenly, like a flash of lightning, *they found themselves free, there were no more problems.*

Why?

Because *the platform of ignorance* the devil had *in their lives* was now taken away from him. He finds himself *without any authority,* no more room to maneuver, *no more place or platform to operate from* **and so he must flee.**

You see, it is quite often the case that things are allowed to dominate our lives, *because we feel that we* **need** *them. And then we deceive ourselves about it and even get to the point of* **seeing nothing wrong with it**, even though it is *negative, degrading forces* at work in our lives, *destructive even*, obscuring and *even distorting* the beauty of our *original design:* **being *the very image and likeness of God*, the very brightness of His glory in a flesh and blood body.**

That ugly thing becomes a *blemish* and a *stain* on the most beautiful masterpiece, **which is YOU!**

It's like a gorgeous bride all dressed up in the choicest hand picked fabrics, but with *spots, blemishes and wrinkles* on that beautiful dress. **To say that this spoils the view and the moment *is an understatement!***

So many of the things *we struggle with,* **or outright deceive ourselves about** and allow in our lives **are symptoms of a spiritual condition. Only partaking of and getting captivated by and saturated with the treasure of righteousness, can cure this condition.**

I dare say most of the things we struggle with *or allow in our lives through self deception* are afforded a place of dominion in our lives through our spiritual *need*, through our spiritual ***starvation for righteousness!***

Those devils only have power as long as they can keep you *self-deceived,* clinging to that *false fulfillment,* or that *alternate identity,* to that *alternative* semi-fulfillment of sin.

*After all, sin does have some pleasure. But the pleasure of sin is short lived and destructive **to the very fabric and being of who you are.***

Those devils only have power as long as they can *keep you ignorant and **keep you from the truth of YOUR righteousness***, as long as they can keep you from ***seeing*** and ***appropriating*** and ***living*** in the *glory* and *the beauty, the pleasure and **the enjoyment and satisfaction and fulfillment of YOUR righteousness.***

Jesus said this:

*"You shall **know** the truth,"*

*"…and (in the knowing of the truth; in the intimate knowing of truth; and in the experience of its REALITY) …**the truth shall make you free**."* - John 8:32

*Once the knowledge of the truth brings the knowledge (the intimate knowledge, and **enjoyment, and treasuring**) of YOUR righteousness, **freedom comes with it**!*

I can also testify that the same thing happened in my life just like it did with many of those who came for counsel. Suddenly **we SAW**:

*'Hey, the devil **lied** to me.'*

*'I don't **need** to be dominated by this stupid, degrading thing anymore;'*

*'I **AM** the righteousness of God. (MY righteousness **is from Him, it's a gift!**)'*

*'I am **accepted** in the beloved, because of my **union** with Christ Jesus, **because He represented me in that work of redemption**.'*

*'I am not accepted because I am relating to God through some set of rules, some law of performance, some philosophy of man, or some man-made religion; some church custom and tradition, but **because my righteousness comes directly from God**.'*

*'It is the righteousness **of God Himself, His very own righteousness given to me as a gift**.'*

That is the only righteousness that God wants us to partake of. *Nothing less, **nothing inferior!*** No lesser righteousness *of our own* *making,* through religion or *trying to uphold a bunch of empty do's and don'ts that we somehow in our heads turned into another Law of God!*

Romans 10:1-4,

1 *"Brethren, my heart's desire and prayer to God, is that they may be saved* (rescued and made whole)..."

He was talking about the Jews, who were a religious people, always busy with a bunch of rather empty do's and don'ts.

 3 *"For they,* **being ignorant of God's righteousness,** *and* (therefore still) *seeking to establish their own righteousness* (through their own efforts and man-made empty religious do's and don'ts), *have not submitted to the righteousness of God..."*

The righteousness under law is not good enough because it is a carnal effort, *man's own efforts through his own ability,* **to try and become acceptable before God.** *It wears you out and exhausts you in every way. It could never bring fulfillment, because it leaves us empty, worn out and wounded* in our own striving, **and it results in all kinds of sin dominating our lives!**

In our own striving under the law, sin ends up dominating our lives **because we are compelled to fill the empty gap within us**

with whatever we think can provide temporary short -lived fulfillment just to soothe our hurting, empty soul. We end up deceiving ourselves and living an empty, hollow shell of a life *because we are driven by spiritual **need** and **starvation.***

Thank God the end of these things is at hand! The light of the world has come and the true light is already shining, and the darkness is passing away!

In these things I am sharing, there is a new day dawning for humanity …and yes, <u>for you</u>! Especially for you who have the privilege of reading <u>these truths</u>!

Let's get back to John 14:3,

"I will come again and receive you to Myself; that where I am, there you may be also."

*"...**you may be also**."*

Begin to imagine that God has in mind for you *to enjoy His presence* **to the same degree that Jesus enjoys the Father's presence!**

Even if you don't believe it fully now, can you at least begin to acknowledge that that *is* what God desires?

All the Scriptures *say so* and we know that they are God *inspired.*

2 Timothy 3:15 & 16,

15 *"...the Holy Scriptures,* **are able to make you wise for salvation** <u>through</u> (the) <u>faith</u> *which is in Christ Jesus…*

16 *All Scripture is given by inspiration of God* (literally God breathed)*, and is profitable for doctrine, for reproof, for correction;* **for instruction in righteousness***…"*

Listen, God wants you to have *such confidence* before Him *that you act like and are like; I mean, it is just like it would be if Jesus Himself were standing there in His Father's presence.*

God wants you to act like and be like that in His presence! He *wants you to* ***feel just*** *as* ***welcome*** *in His presence as Jesus feels* ***welcome*** *in His presence.*

So, you don't need to wear a mask or come with some pretense, or some religious cliché. But you can just come, knowing you can come, *having confidence that you belong there!*

You belong in your Daddy's presence.

Chapter 4

The Way, The Truth, and The Life

Okay, now here in this Scripture Jesus Himself is saying,

*"I will come and receive you to Myself, that **where I am, <u>there</u> you may be also.**"*

– John 14:3

Where is this place He is talking about?

The answer lies right here in the next few verses,

4 *"And <u>you know the way</u> where I am going.*

5 *Thomas said to Him, 'Lord we do not know where You are going, <u>how do we **know** the way</u>?'*

6 *Jesus said to him, 'I am the way, and the truth, and the life; no one comes to the Father, but through Me.'*

7 *'If you had known Me, you would have known My Father also;'*

*'...**from now on you know Him and have seen Him.**'*

8 Phillip said to Him, 'Lord, show us the Father, and it is enough for us.'

9 Jesus said to him, 'Have I been so long with you, and yet you have not come to know Me, Philip?'

*'**He who has seen Me has seen the Father; how do you say: 'Show us the Father?'***

*10 **Do you not believe** that **I am <u>in</u> the Father**, and **the Father is <u>in</u> Me?***

*The words that I say to you I do not speak on My own initiative, but **the Father <u>abiding in</u> Me** does His works.*

*11 Believe Me that I am **in** the Father, and the Father is **in** Me, otherwise believe on account of the works themselves."*

- John 14:4-11(NRSV)

Thomas suddenly realized that it was crucial for him *to **know** <u>the way</u>*. *'I mean, what if I'm not around when He comes, what if I miss His coming!'* He was afraid that he would miss out because Jesus said *He was going away and then coming again to take them to the place where He is.*

This is how Jesus answered him. He said,

'There is no other way Phillip, you can't get there on your own. It's not a natural place, no physical address, so there are no directions I can give you. There's no step 1, step 2, step 3.'

Look at Verse 6 where He said,

*"**I am the way**, and **the truth**, and **the life**. No one comes to the Father except through Me (**through believing the things I am saying about my work of redemption**)."*

When you begin to see this truth of *__YOUR righteousness__*, you begin to realize what Jesus meant when He said these things. You begin to realize that *it's impossible for mankind to relate to God **as Father**, except through this revelation of __righteousness__ **given to us as a gift in the work of redemption, actually restored to us** in the death of Jesus on our behalf*.

*It is rightfully OURS. It has been OURS all along. We lost it in the garden through Adam. **We lost sight of it through ignorance and empty deception**, but it is OURS and it is now being restored to us **by Jesus, by the Father Himself, in this work of redemption!***

It doesn't matter how religiously devoted to your specific religion you are, or what religious philosophy you cling to. It doesn't matter whether it is Christianity, Islam, Hinduism, Buddhism, Mormonism, Jehovah's Witness,

New Age, or Humanism, or simply being a good person, *or whatever other philosophies there may be out there, numerous as they may be.* **There is no philosophy that you can cling to that has in it the legal integrity able to restore mankind to God.**

It took God Himself, incarnate, in the man Jesus Christ, to restore us back to Himself.

You see, *God didn't have religion in mind.* No, God has **companionship** in mind with Man.

God has an intimate relationship of love in mind for mankind ...and <u>no</u> religion whatsoever (Not even the religion of Christianity outside of this revelation of **OUR righteousness restored**) has in it *the ability to so restore mankind to God* **in true fellowship, to where there is no longer any sense of sin, and of guilt. To where <u>every trace of it is removed</u>!**

This kind of relationship, *available to you* **through Jesus' death on your behalf,** is not something fake, something false. **It is real, it is truth; it's no lie.**

Let me say it in another way: If you suffer from cancer in your body *and take tranquilizers, the cancer is still there, even though you don't feel it or worry about it anymore.* **That, my friend is exactly what the religious traditions of men offer you: deception and self-delusion!**

The problem with religion is that *the cancer remains.* Religious doctrines and teachings all work like tranquilizers. And tranquilizers may make you stop thinking and worrying about the pain, and can even get you to overlook your cancer for a while. But no amount of tranquilizers *can stop the cancer from eating you up inside.*

The Church of the Lord Jesus Christ was never meant to preach doctrines *that promote that kind of* **self-delusional thought process.** Those inaccurate doctrines and teachings are *full of subtle lies* and are inspired by the enemy, *keeping people in bondage, deceiving them.*

Satan has many sincere Christians in bondage by these kinds of *doctrines of demons.* They might even preach many other things that are wholesome and right, but without an accurate emphasis on our restored original righteousness, there is a lot of teaching that, *even though it sounds good, even though it sounds right,* <u>*it is interwoven with inaccurate doctrines promoting weakness*</u>. **And because of that there can be no release, and <u>the people remain in bondage</u>.**

"How can a blind man lead the blind? They will all fall into a pit of darkness," Jesus said in Matthew 15:14.

The Scriptures also say, when speaking of the deceptive teachings of the religious people, that, *"…a little leaven will leaven the whole lump." It will cause us to remain in bondage.*

Those doctrines and teachings *make subtle excuses for sin while emphasizing works,* and therefore it will *steal your freedom.*

If we mix our freedom *with a little bondage, that little bit of bondage is still bondage, and will turn our whole freedom into bondage.*

Listen, the Gospel is not just some tranquilizing tablet *for your nerves, to calm your fears and soothe your guilty conscience to silence* by the grace of God, by His mercy and His abounding love, *even though you continue to live in darkness!* That is not what the grace of God represents! That is an inaccurate representation of all that Jesus died for! We cannot afford to buy into such an inferior representation of the grace of God!

We need to get rid of those old Sunday-school doctrines which have caged us in and limited our understanding to mansions in the sky and freedom only one day in Heaven when Jesus comes again, *instead of seeing what God actually has in mind.*

It is astounding how, *just like the Jews of old,* people everywhere love to hold on to those wrong little pet doctrines and teachings:

'I've always believed it this way ever since I was little, and I am not about to change now!'

'I'll just keep on believing it my way. *I don't care how you see it brother Rudi, I see it this way.'*

Well, they can just keep on seeing it their way, but I'm telling you, **they'll remain in bondage.**

God wants us to be *released,* **to be totally released** into a dimension of encounter and life that is so large *that it surpasses knowledge.* It surpasses our little pet doctrines and teachings which **make excuses for our weaknesses** *and hold us in bondage.*

Hey man, don't limit God in your walk with Him. Don't tie God's hands through your stubborn refusal *to see the truth clearly,* your stubborn refusal to be *persuaded!* I beg of you, *don't settle for a lesser life than what God has in mind for us all,* by stubbornly clinging to your pet religious little doctrines and teachings of *deception and lies!*

Don't tie God's hands and prevent Him from *bringing you* **fully** *into that place of* **liberty** *and* **victory** *He prepared for* **YOU**!

God wants YOU,

…*legally* …literally;

*…to partake of **abundant life in HIM!***

Can you believe that?

Do you believe that *today, this very day, you can live **a maximum life!? Not an inferior life, but a maximum life in Him and through Him!?***

The Scripture says in another place, *"Today while you hear God's voice, do not harden your hearts!"*

In Verse 7 of John 14 Jesus said,

"If you had known Me, you would have known My Father also.

***From now on you know Him, and have seen Him**.*"

Phillip, also still not understanding that, through Jesus' words and in His actions, **He was revealing to them the deepest thoughts and desires of God the Father towards mankind,** said to Him,

"Lord, show us the Father and we will be satisfied."

He didn't understand that seeing God in the natural would not have satisfied them as much as what Jesus was revealing to them about the Father and about what He was about to do for THEM and for US. The understanding that Jesus brought to them, ***revealing the Father's heart and revealing***

what He was about to accomplish was exactly what they ***needed.*** **Those truths, that revelation *was more than enough to satisfy them.***

In Verse 9 we see Jesus' disappointed response to their dullness of hearing, their failure to perceive, their lack of insight and comprehension, their failure to receive.

"Jesus said to him,

'Have I been with you so long and yet you have not come to know Me, Phillip?'

'How can you dare say; 'Show us the Father?'

*'He who has seen Me <u>**has seen**</u> the Father."*

Paul says,

*"Even though once we regarded Him **after the flesh,** (from a natural, human point of view)"*

He says,

"We have all failed to see the hidden message and hidden work of God on our behalf in this man…"

"But now we regard Him thus no longer."

- 2 Corinthians 5:16

"Who do men say that I am?" Jesus once asked.

"Well maybe He's a prophet, maybe He's this or that...'

"But who do you say that I am?"

And by the Spirit of God, by revelation (insight into a secret, insight into the hidden message of God) Peter said,

"You are the Christ (the Messiah **sent to die for our sin and to free us from our sins and give us back our righteousness**)*..."*

"You are the Son of the living God (the One who represents and accurately exhibits the living God; ***His exact image and precise likeness on display***)*."*

- Matthew 16:13

*"Phillip, have I been with you so long **and yet you have not seen the Father**."*

- John 14:9.

What is Jesus saying?

"...where I am you may be also."

You see, if Phillip *couldn't* **see or comprehend** the **unity,** the **oneness** between Jesus and His Father, *he would* **fail to receive** what Jesus was saying to him. Before Phillip could ***receive or enter into*** that place that Jesus was talking to him about, ***he had to first understand*** *Jesus' righteousness. He had to first **see and understand** the **unity**, the **oneness** between Jesus and His Father!*

I want to emphasize this point again: **If we don't understand Jesus' righteousness, if we don't understand the completeness of His union with His Father, we will fail to comprehend the completeness of the unity available to US. We will fail to understand God's plan and purpose for our lives, *accomplished in Christ.***

Jesus was not only the revelation of what God wants mankind to enjoy as far as intimacy is concerned, but He was also *a revelation of God's purpose for mankind,* God's plan and desire ***to reveal everything concerning Himself and relating to man, in and through US, through our very lives.***

Verse 10 reveals the answer to the question:

Jesus where are You?

What is this place You're talking about?

He said,

*"Do you not believe that **I AM IN MY FATHER AND THE FATHER IN ME**?"*

In the natural mindset we would be tempted to think that Jesus was going to give away His address now so we could go and visit Him as often as we would want to. But no, **He was talking in spirit dimension.**

Through His words he was revealing to them *where He truly lives and dwells constantly.* And it's not some geographical place, somewhere in outer space (I do believe that Heaven is a literal place *in spirit dimension, <u>but occupying and enjoying our place in the Father</u> doesn't have to wait* till we one day go to Heaven).

In other words, Jesus said,

"I am going to show you the way, so you can get there."

"I'm going to reveal to you the truth. And by that truth, **the life I now enjoy, the life that you were also created for,** *you will also <u>now</u> be able to enjoy and **live** through the truth."*

"Through the truth (understanding into God's true purpose and plan)*, you will be able to know the way to get there* (the place designed for you)*,"*

"…so you can get there;"

*"…so you can get to **where I am;**"*

*"…so you can **be** where I **am;**"*

"…so you would no longer be troubled, thinking, 'Oh, I wonder what happened to Jesus. He died over two thousand years ago, and now we are still desolate as orphans, desperately just trying our best to hang in there waiting for His return, by which He's going to deliver us and give us an escape from this crooked and perverse generation ...oh, we just can't wait for Jesus to come back...'

*'Oh… Jesus please come back quickly, **before we all get sucked in by the wickedness of this world**.'*

I know what Jesus' response to that kind of defeated thinking would be:

*'Listen man, **you may be where I am**,'*

*'YOU MAY BE **WHERE I AM**!'*

'So that 'times of refreshing may come directly from the very presence of the Lord Himself. Amen!'

Times of refreshing may <u>now</u> come to us in the presence of the Lord!

The fullness of time <u>*has*</u> already (past tense) fully come.

John 14:10,

*"...<u>Believe</u> that I am **in** the Father and the Father **in** Me."*

We need spirit perception; **faith,** *to value this truth, this **reality**.*

"The words that I speak to you are spirit and they are life."

"I do not speak them on My own authority (or my own initiative even);"

*"...but the Father Himself **who dwells in Me and with Me** does these works."*

Isaiah 50:4 & 5 say about Jesus,

4 *"The Lord God has given Me the tongue of the learned, just as the pen of a ready writer, that I should know how to sustain with the Word him who is weary."*

Morning by morning He awakens My ear to hear as the learned,

5 *yes He has opened My ear and so I was not rebellious."*

This is a prophetic picture out of Isaiah's inspired writings that has hidden in it *the revelation of the dwelling that Jesus has with His Father.* He, as a man, was talking out of His relationship with His Father and His God.

"He gave me the tongue exercised in speaking His Word."

He wasn't speaking out of some theological school background. He wasn't speaking the knowledge that just puffs up and promotes the pride of life, bondage, tradition, and dead works.

His words were spirit and life, fresh from the presence of God, from out of His union with God. He was speaking forth thoughts that He was intimately sharing with God, thoughts inspired by the heart of God Himself.

John 1:18 says,

"The only begotten…"

(The **MONOGENES** – ORIGINAL, **BEGOTTEN ONLY OF GOD,** AUTHENTIC BLUEPRINT SON; the ORIGINAL BLUEPRINT of both man and God; the son of man and the Son of God; **this ORIGINAL AUTHENTIC BLUEPRINT <u>SON</u>**,)

"…who <u>is</u> in the bosom of the Father,"

"HE HAS REVEALED HIM."

God wants you and me to minister *from the intimacy of our relationship with Him*, to speak *out of* that place. He wants our ministry not to be just some memorized approach *that we have learned in the classroom,* but **to be the overflow of the life that we enjoy within ourselves in fellowship with Father God.**

That kind of ministry will make such a real, undeniable difference.

This revelation of your original righteousness restored releases you *to fellowship to such a degree with Jesus* that **out of the abundance of the heart** a <u>river</u> *will begin to flow* that will *touch* people's *lives*, not because of your clever persuasive method of words, **but because of the demonstration, the manifestation of Spirit and power.**

Listen, any man out there *can tell the difference* between a neat little method and, oh it can be such a neat approach, *so well polished.* Devils *can definitely tell the difference* between a neat little method **and the words that I hear in the closet, the revelation I receive in my spirit because I dwell with Jesus,** in *intimate fellowship with Him.*

I can just hear Jesus say,

'*My little children,* **this is where I am**,'

'...**this is where I dwell**,'

'...**in intimate fellowship with Him**'

'...**and I'm bringing you into it**,'

'...<u>**so that you may do My works and greater**</u>.'

Greater?

Yes, greater!

Jesus and Peter both raised the dead, but, wasn't Peter's shadow healing people simply as he walked down the street *a greater work* than a woman touching the hem of Jesus' garment?

Sure it was!

Also, Jesus' works were limited to one individual body at that time. But there would be a multiplication of bodies (people, us) *that would be linked up together with God and with one another in the Spirit, in spirit dimension,* to become the vehicle, the Church of the living God, *so that a multiplication of His words and works might put the devil to flight everywhere here on planet earth!*

Do you see God's strategy? God is beginning, in this revelation to reveal to you that you have a part in His strategy. But before you can begin to see your part, you first *need* to *begin to see* your place in Him. **God wants you to see your place in Him.** Amen?!

Back to John 14:10,

"...the words that I speak to you, I do not speak on My own authority (in My own initiative).*"*

What would Jesus' own authority be linked to? It would be linked to His *natural identity*. I am talking about His *personality,* His *natural talents,* His *education,* His *social status,* His *natural image* and His *skill,* that He could seek to enhance and portray to the world.

But He said, and listen carefully now, He said,

'I don't put confidence in My own authority, but **My confidence is in the authority I am allowed to operate in through My righteousness, <u>through the relationship that I walk in with God.</u>***'*

'*I walk in an intimate, transparent, love relationship with Him.***'**

If you begin to understand <u>what God has in mind with righteousness</u> you will begin to abhor and detest every opportunity for sin.

Sin (missing the mark; living outside of what you were designed for), and the temptation to sin, *will lose its attraction to you* **because that which is more excellent will be revealed to your heart.**

And then, listen, you can clearly begin to tell the difference *between dung and gold.*

Sin is just a sugarcoated pill of poison. It is at best just dung that is gold-plated.

When you begin to discover *the real thing,* not religion, **the real thing** (the ability that YOU have as a human being to stand in the presence of the Creator God and to *know Him* and *fellowship with Him* **as Father, as your Daddy**) ...hey, **THAT'S gold. That's value, that's treasure beyond price.**

Can you begin to appreciate the precious blood of Jesus? Can you begin to appreciate what it cost Him *to give to you and me the opportunity* ***that He has?*** *To bring you and I into the privilege* ***that He has*** *to relate to Father God* **as His own Father, without a sense of inferiority!?**

He wants us, you and I, to relate to Father God, **Our Father,** *with that same revelation, that same knowledge in our hearts,* **that same sense of innocence and equality.**

Jesus was preparing a place **for US** and furthermore, He wants us to **understand** that **there will come, there will be, an indwelling of God within us, an indwelling!**

John 14:10,

"...but **the Father who dwells in Me***, does the works."*

Do you now see that *mere man-made religious philosophy* **could never give man this opportunity?**

But Jesus, *through His sacrificial death*, *could so blot out **the power and dominion of sin*** *in man's life, He could so blot out **the memory of sin and guilt*** *that He could again **become the way*** *for mankind to approach the Father **in righteousness,** through Him,* **through the torn veil of His broken flesh!**

Chapter 5

I Will Send the Helper to You

11 *"Believe Me **that I am in the Father** and **the Father in Me**; otherwise believe on account of the works themselves.*

12 *Truly, truly* (most assuredly), *I say to you, he who believes in Me, **the works that I do shall he do also**; and greater works than these shall he do; **because I go to the Father**.*

13 *And whatever you ask in My name, **that will I do**, that the Father may be glorified in the Son.*

14 *If you ask Me anything in My name, **I will do it**.*

15 *If you love Me **you will keep** (believe and embrace and value) My commandments;*

16 *and I will ask the Father, and He will give you another* (Comforter; another) ***Helper*** (ENCOURAGER, FRIEND, INSPIRATION), ***that He may be with you** (abide with you) **forever**."*

- John 14:11-16 (NASV)

For the first time now Jesus introduces the Holy Spirit. The word '**Comforter**' or '*Helper*' used here in the original language is the word **PARACLETOS,** which comes from two Greek words:

PARA – a preposition indicating CLOSE PROXIMITY, PROCEEDING FROM a sphere of influence, suggesting A UNION OF PLACE OF RESIDENCE, having ORIGINATED and COME FORTH FROM ITS AUTHOR AND GIVER, it is denoting the point FROM WHICH an action ORIGINATES, INTIMATE CONNECTION,

And the word: **KALEO** – TO IDENTIFY, TO RECOGNIZE PERSONALLY BY NAME, TO SURNAME.

The word '*Helper*' means ONE WHO COMES ALONG-SIDE. ONE WHO'S CALLED ALONG-SIDE TO HELP, TO ENCOURAGE; TO INSPIRE, *TO BE A FRIEND (Just like Jesus was to His disciples).*

That influence that would come, to call you, *to draw you,* to bring you *into* what Jesus prepared for you, is *the Spirit of Truth,* or Holy Spirit. It is the same resurrected Spirit of Jesus Himself.

That Spirit of Truth, that resurrected Spirit of Jesus Christ is holy and pure and full of love, belonging exclusively to the Father and the Son, and now to us also.

Listen, we will not understand the ministry of the Spirit of Truth, of the Holy Spirit through us, before *we first understand our* **union with Him,** *OUR* **righteousness.**

We also need to understand the word *'another'* as it is used here in, *'***ANOTHER Helper***'* There are two different words for *'another'* in the original language.

This word *'another'* (OR **ALOS**) means: ANOTHER OF THE SAME KIND. The other word: *'another'* (OR **HETEROS**) means ANOTHER OF A DIFFERENT KIND.

When we speak of **another of a different kind** it is like two different books, one a novel and the other a history book. Even though they are both books, the one is *uniquely different from the other*.

Speaking in *"OTHER TONGUES"* (1 Corinthians 14) is also a superb example of the usage of the word for **another of a different kind**. The languages of the world are all languages **of the same kind** (ALOS), so even though you are German and speaking in *another* (ALOS) language, like English, you are still speaking **an earthly language**, a language **of the same kind** (ALOS).

But now, even though speaking in *"OTHER TONGUES"* is speaking in a language, it is from the Spirit, it is from above (Heavenly), it is a language **of a different kind, of another**

kind (HETEROS) *not related to the languages of this world.*

When I say, *"OTHER TONGUES"* is a language **of a different kind or of another kind** (HETEROS) *not related to the languages of this world,* I am not talking about the manifestation of the corporate gift of *"speaking in tongues" (*or a better phraseology would be *"giving a message in tongues").*

Sometimes during meetings people speak forth a message in **other** (HETEROS) **tongues** from the Holy Spirit, and sometimes people supernaturally speak forth a message in **other** (ALOS) **tongues without realizing they are speaking in another known language.**

They spoke out, as far as they were concerned in **other** (HETEROS) **tongue**s. But **supernaturally** they spoke out in **another** (ALOS) **understandable earthly language** which they themselves have not learned and do not know how to speak naturally, but which someone else in the congregation can either understand, or both understand and speak.

Of course, if they speak out a message in **other** (HETEROS) **tongues** from the Holy Spirit, then there also needs to be a **supernatural interpretation** of those **other** (HETEROS) **tongues** for the congregation to understand what was said and be encouraged by it (See 1 Corinthians 14 and Acts 2).

When Jesus spoke of *"**another Helper**",* He was using the word (ALOS), that speaks of ***another of the exact same kind*** (like two New King James Bibles).

Do you see it? ***Do you see the unity between Jesus and the Holy Spirit? The Holy Spirit is not another of a different kind, He is another of the exact same kind.***

They are the same! The same content, the same value, the One is not worth less than the other One. The Holy Spirit is just like Jesus, and He is just like the Father. It would be just like having Jesus still with them, but NOW IN THEM.

When you begin to view the Holy Spirit ***in this light,*** **you will be unable to view Him as an inferior partner to God.** You will stop longing so much to be in Heaven somewhere with Jesus, and you will start realizing that *He (Jesus) is not only with you, but you can enjoy His presence* **fully in the NOW. *You can have the same fullness of fellowship with Him as He has with Father God right now!***

The Holy Spirit is the One **who practically ministers to our spirits** *the legal **reality** of OUR place, prepared **just for us**, in Christ Jesus. **He practically administers to our spirits the very glory of God, the very presence of God.***

John 14:16 & 17,

"My PARACLETOS, Another, **the exact same as I am***, even* **the Spirit of Truth (Who represents <u>My reality</u>, the <u>reality</u> of God Himself);"**

"…whom the world cannot receive, <u>because it neither sees Him, nor knows Him</u>;"

"But you know Him, **for He <u>dwells</u> with you (while I'm with you, He is already here IN ME, He dwells with you now already)** *and <u>will be in you</u>, Him will I send <u>in My place</u>."*

"I've been with you so long and yet do you not <u>know</u> Me?"

"He dwells with you already, in My presence with you, He dwells with you, **BUT** *He will be* **in you.***"*

Jesus is preparing His disciples for *that new dimension,* **that new realm of experience,** *that will now be available* after his death, resurrection, and ascension, because He goes to prepare a place for fallen Man. **And then the Holy Spirit, the resurrected Spirit of Jesus and of the Father Himself, will come** *to administrate that truth,* **not just by being with us,** *but by coming to dwell <u>in us!</u>*

We cannot even begin to understand what Colossians 1:27, *"****Christ <u>in you</u>****, the hope of glory"* **<u>truly</u> means** if we fail to understand the ministry and the work of the Holy Spirit. **By revealing the truth, <u>eternal reality</u>, to us, He brings the <u>reality</u> of Christ's <u>indwelling</u> into our spirits, so that we may encounter and enjoy His glory and His presence and His <u>reality</u> there in our spirits, in the here and now.**

John 14:18,

"I will not leave you desolate (as orphans)*, **I will come to you**."*

In other words, He was saying to His disciples,

"You don't need to be troubled. You're not going to be left in a vacuum, stuck with only a historical reference of a Jesus who lived an incredible life and died a sad death, and rose again and left, and now you are looking forward with bated breath to His soon return, while in the mean time remaining desolate, unfulfilled, as orphans.'

"No! You will be able to <u>relate</u>, in present tense revelation, to the <u>reality</u> of the One who <u>lives</u>, who is <u>I AM</u>."

The best religion can offer is just a vacuum experience, a tremendous history and a glorious hope, but void, nothing in-between in the present day experience.

'Something happened over 2000 years ago now, and something might happen in the

future...' And that is about as much as you know, and you live in the dark and in ignorance and deception, and you're groping around in the meantime in philosophies and endless genealogies and vague prophecies and arguments and stale old man-made religious church doctrines.

But God wants to release to you NOW <u>the full understanding</u> of the New Covenant relationship with Him.

This is something *so precious, <u>so holy</u>*. I don't want us to miss it.

If you miss this revelation, you might as well not try and learn anything else in the Scriptures, **for it will just be powerless to you. It will become confusing and empty doctrines.**

We are not called to serve Jesus or go out and preach the gospel ***because of religious duty.***

To me there is nothing attractive to Christianity *outside of this truth of righteousness.*

There is nothing attractive to my walk with Jesus *outside of this reality.*

This truth and this reality of **MY righteousness** *is what gives it all its attraction.* **This truth and reality of HAVING *the same righteousness* as Jesus, the Son of God, is the very root of my fulfillment and satisfaction. It's the very**

root of <u>reality with God</u>, the root of true intimate friendship and fellowship with God, and with my fellow human beings I share this planet with.

God doesn't want us to be fasting, giving, praying, or anything else **because of a sense of religious duty.**

Rather, He wants **the fruit** of this revelation; **our hearts burning with passion and desire, our hearts burning with His love for us as well as for the rest of mankind**... **He wants THAT to be the thing that is burning in our hearts!** And He wants *that burning* <u>to be the source</u> of our fasting, praying and everything else.

Paul said, *"Woe to me if I preach not the GOSPEL* (the Good News)*,"* because he had a revelation **into this truth of righteousness <u>and its fruit</u>!**

He knew there was nothing else, no other revelation that could bring *true satisfaction, true fulfillment, true intimate fellowship;* **REALITY to our walk with God.**

Everything else ends up being the dead works of religion.

Paul confirms this in other places:

*"**Therefore** if* (since – it's a conclusion not a condition) *any man is in Christ,* ***he IS a new creation***..." - 2 Corinthians 5:17

"I'm crucified (together) *<u>with Christ</u>,* (my old empty, sinful, lost, self) *nevertheless I live,* (my new creation, redeemed, and restored to my original design, self) **yet not I,** *but* **<u>it is Christ</u> (that very image and likeness of Christ; that blueprint design of the Christ-life, yes,** *even that very Spirit of the resurrected Christ Himself***)** **that <u>lives</u> and <u>dwells</u> and <u>abides</u> in me.**" - Galatians 2:20

"...*Christ **<u>lives</u> in me**.*"

That is awesome! I tell you, **ministry itself becomes a drag** *if you don't have this revelation.*

Sacrifice becomes so costly *when you don't have this revelation.*

Comfort becomes so valuable and attractive *when you don't have this revelation.*

But let me tell you, **hardship, tribulation, the price of ministry becomes your glory** *in this revelation.*

Paul said,

"I glory in tribulation."

Why?

Because he found access *into the kind of relationship* from which no amount of tribulation, no sized persecution, no height, nor depth, nothing, could separate him. Nothing could separate him from the revelation of God *who comes to **dwell** within*.

Romans 8:31,

*"**If** (since – it is a conclusion, not a condition) **God is for me**, who can be against me?"*

1John 4:4,

*"Greater is **He who is in you** than he who is in the world."*

I want you to know **it's a costly thing to follow Jesus *and only within this revelation do you find the strength, the courage to do it.*** And do not kid yourself: There is a high price to pay in the flesh. People will persecute you for His name's sake.

In the book of Acts we read about Stephen's life and his stoning in the flesh, *but he partook of incorruptible life in the spirit.* He walked in the place that Jesus prepared for him. He was not left desolate, without strength. No! That persecution couldn't rob from him his life. **Nothing could interrupt it, amen?!**

Can you see in this passage of John 14 how *Jesus continues to give them **substance for***

their faith in order to destroy their fears, in order to calm their troubled hearts?

Can you see that in this revelation, *in the light of **YOUR righteousness**, in the light of such tremendous **love and embrace and acceptance** by Jesus and the Father,* **all basis for fear is removed!?**

Not even death can bring fear. Even the sting of death is removed.

"Oh death, where is your sting?"

*'So what if they kill me, **I'm just going to continue to <u>dwell</u> <u>with</u> <u>Him</u> who now satisfies me** and comforts me and calms my heart and removes all my fears!'*

*"**Because I live**, you will **live** also... I am **the resurrection** and the **life**,"* Jesus said, *"I will not leave you desolate, **I will come to you.**"*

And now in John 14, Verse 19 He says,

*"A little while longer and the world will see Me no more, **<u>but you will see Me</u>** because I **live**, you will **live** also. <u>In that day</u> you will **<u>KNOW</u>** that I am <u>in My Father</u> and you <u>in Me</u> and <u>I in you</u>."*

How will we know? **Because <u>we will be there also</u>.**

Remember, Jesus already said that, *"He is **IN** His Father"* in verse 10. **He already gave us His address. He lives there,** *in His Father's love.* **He** belongs **there. He** dwells **there** *in His Father's bosom* **for all eternity** *in that place.*

But now, here in Verse 19 He brings in the dimension of **life** available to the believer in the New Covenant:

"And you in Me and I in you."

And in 15:10:

"Abide in My love."

Do you see the plan for the fullness of time? Can you see the plan, the mystery being unfolded to those men, **and now to the hearts of all mankind,** through this passage from the Bible?

Jesus was clothed with the robe of righteousness, *His spirit was clothed in righteousness.* And they stripped Him naked, but they didn't do it, they couldn't. He put it aside.

He said,

"No man takes My life from Me, I put it aside."

He didn't even consider it robbery to be in this flesh and blood body while being equal with

God. He enjoyed oneness with the Father. But even though He enjoyed absolute unity with God, **He willingly laid equality aside** ***to become sin for us.*** He became naked **with your nakedness.** He took upon Himself **the nakedness** that Adam and Eve had to face ***when they were stripped of the glory of God, when they no longer had the consciousness of righteousness in their spirits.***

Adam and Eve felt *the* **fear** and *the* **guilt** and they were **condemned,** they were **naked,** they could no longer *stand* **face-to-face**, they lost **equality,** they could no longer **face Him**.

But Jesus took that *nakedness,* that *shame* upon Himself, when He *emptied* Himself upon that cross, in order **to clothe us again!**

Oh what a sacrifice, what an unthinkable act of love *to give all that up <u>for us</u>:* **His beautiful robe of** *righteousness*, **so that <u>we</u> could be made** *partakers of His righteousness,* **of His** *Divine nature*, **of His** *very glory!* **That's the place He prepared for us. He prepared for us that robe of** *righteousness.* **And it's not a robe you put on,** *it's one you put <u>in</u> through understanding these things, through faith, through understanding and believing <u>your</u> redemption! He clothes your spirit with <u>righteousness</u>.*

1 Corinthians 6:17 says,

*"He who is **joined** to the Lord,* (**totally united, completely one** with the Lord) *is <u>one spirit with Him</u>."*

If you are joined to the Lord, dear friend, ***then you ARE <u>completely united</u> with Him, <u>one spirit with Him</u>!***

What joins us *in a REAL and practical way* **to the Lord, not just in some vague spiritual concept?**

It's the **abiding** word, the **abiding** Truth of *our <u>righteousness</u> given to us in redemption.* It's **His abiding love,** His **abiding Spirit of Truth,** His **abiding Spirit of faith,** the **Holy Spirit** who comes to ***confirm*** and ***establish*** *us in faith,* who comes to ***confirm*** and ***<u>establish the truth</u> in our inner man*** *when we hear the Word of Truth, the Gospel of OUR **salvation**, of OUR **righteousness** through Him!*

*Let this truth **ABIDE**. Let this abiding truth **renew your mind**.* **Turn away from** *the thought processes* **inherited from this blind, blind, world.** *Turn away from any lie you held on to through religion and tradition,* ***because THIS IS TRUTH, the only LIBERATING TRUTH! Embrace THIS TRUTH, <u>believe it fully</u>, and you'll discover a freedom like you've never had before.***

This world would like you to wear masks all the time, and they want to force you to do it, because they wouldn't accept you unless you think like them and talk like them and act like them, and do this and do that. They won't accept you unless you wear that mask, and at least pretend to agree with them and be like them, even if you don't agree with them and do not consider yourself to be like them. You've got to be phony, because you want to be accepted. You feel so naked, you feel so lonely, so isolated, and you want to be accepted, *so you do all these funny, stupid things just so that people would like you.*

Listen, if you are a Christian, don't take that junk into your fellowship with one another.

God wants you to walk *open and transparent* before Him. And when God **sets your heart free,** through faith, through truth, to relate to Him, then *suddenly you find yourself **free** to relate to your brothers and sisters **in a new way** as well.*

You no longer **need** masks of any kind. You no longer *need* **to be** phony, to be fake, to be liked, you can just **be** yourself **(Your New Creation self, not the old, ignorant, sinful self).** You can just **be** that original design in which He has made you to be: His image, His likeness, His love **on display!** You are just **free** to be your true self, to exhibit your true identity **as child of God!**

We no longer need to regard each other from a human point of view, but *we begin to see the quality and the identity of the New Creature*. We see *that identity of being sons of God!*

And in our fellowship we promote the coming forth of that identity out of one another because it is already in us just as surely as we are the image and likeness of God, just as surely as we are partakers of the Divine nature, just as surely as we are the children of God!

That is what we promote in our fellowship with one another: Our true design restored and awakened in Jesus Christ's work of redemption, and <u>in our hearing of it, and our BELIEVING</u> *that truth*.

John 14:20 says,

*"You will **<u>know</u>**…"*

That little word '***know***' in the original language is the word **EPIGNOSIS,** and it means **TO INTIMATELY KNOW, TO FULLY KNOW.**

*"You will **<u>know</u>** …"*

*"…**that I am <u>in My Father</u> and you <u>in Me</u> and <u>I in you</u>.**"*

Chapter 6

If You've Seen Me, You've Seen the Father

Jesus said,

*"I am in My Father, **if you've seen Me, you've seen the Father.**"*

For too long religion has painted us the wrong picture of the Father. We grew up thinking that Jesus is a little less strict than the Father because we were taught in such a way about God that we got the idea that the Father is some stern old person sitting there in Heaven on His throne with a big stick, *ready to beat us!*

But I want you to know that *when you've seen Jesus, **you've seen the Father**.* Amen?!

When Jesus forgave that woman caught in the act of adultery, **it was the Father who forgave her.**

Sometimes we can be tempted to think that God wasn't quite in agreement with Jesus when He made that decision, *but only if we don't understand **their unity** in relationship.*

It could be easy for us to think together with those Pharisees:

'Jesus what are you doing? Don't you know that God still relates to us according to the law?'

'Don't you know He still has the law on His mind and is saying, 'Listen, this woman needs to be stoned?!'

'What are you doing now Jesus?!'

Can you see with me? *The Father **revealed His Word** through His Son.*

The Father spoke His own words through the lips of His Son when he released that woman from that prison of guilt and condemnation and fear and sin.

When that woman caught in the act of adultery was dragged in before Jesus, *He didn't condemn her,* **but He actually <u>released</u> her** and said, *"**Go and sin no more**."*

Jesus wouldn't have said to her, *"go and sin no more"* if it wasn't possible!

He didn't say, *"go and try to sin a little less, or at least try to hide it a little better!"* No, He said to her in essence, *"**In this act of KINDNESS and LOVE, in this embrace by the Father,** you have received enough **substance** to free you to go and sin no more!"*

I want you to see this clearly: The forgiveness of Jesus, that love, was released to her *with the intention of causing her **to go and sin no more**, He **released** her.*

It is no good for us to just say, *'Well, praise God, I'm forgiven,'* **but we still continue in sin. A person that lives that way has not understood the purpose and intention of God in forgiveness. They have not grasped the love of God! He intends to set us absolutely free from sin by satisfying us with His amazing love,** *not give us a license to continue in sin.*

Listen, don't accommodate sin and make excuses for it in your life!

I am telling you that you can speak in other tongues, you can even sit in meetings listening to messages being preached, or read books just like this one, just as powerful and life changing; ***but if you are deliberately walking in sin, you're canceling out everything that Jesus died for, practically, in your own life,*** *and God's love and forgiveness* ***has almost no effect upon you, and where do you think that leaves you if you continue to trample the precious blood and love of Christ underfoot?***

You are in self-destruct mode, **near to destruction!** That is some sorry state of being my friend.

And I'm not saying that now you better watch out *because now God is going to reject you and destroy you!*

That is not His heart!

His heart is for salvation and deliverance!

He wants to rescue you out of that self-destruct mode!

Listen, sin still has its own wage. It has its own payout, and its payout is death! *Sin specializes in steal, kill and destroy!*

I say again: Do not tolerate sin in your life or you will reap its consequences!

I thank God that fear is no longer a part of the equation in our relationship with God!

God has not given us a spirit of fear, **but of power, and of love, and of a sound mind.**

"For we have not received the spirit of bondage again to fear, but we have received the Spirit of adoption;

…whereby we cry, ABBA, Father, or DADDY." – Romans 8:15

1 John 4:18 & 19 also makes it clear,

"There is no fear in love, but perfect love casts out all fear, **because fear involves torment.**

*He who fears **has not been made perfect in love;***

We love Him because He first loved us!"

We are commissioned to make known the love of God in all its fullness, *so that you may also fall in love with Him and be filled with all the fullness of God.*

Only as we fully grasp and believe the love God has for us *can we develop a true reverence for God that is not fear based but love based.*

And only in that reverence and adoration of God, who is love, do we come into an intimate relationship with Him *as Daddy.*

I say again, *our relationship with Him is not based on fear but on love.* God doesn't want a law or fear-based relationship with you *because that is almost no relationship at all.* It is at best a very shallow relationship because it has distance and separation built into it, *and that is not what God had in mind for us.*

We love Him *because He first loved us!*

Listen, settle it in your heart, God is not the one who comes to destroy in your life! God is not out to get you!

But, at the same time, you cannot live in sin and self destruct mode and think you will get away with it! Sin, not God, will destroy you! Sin is destructive, and evil! It's Candy-coated poison! It is of the Devil!

Listen, you need to understand this *so you can see sin for what it truly is.* I say again: *Sin still pays a wage!* It comes to *steal,* and *destroy,* and *kill*... and that's no joke!

That is why God wants it out of your life! That is why He won't tolerate it if you put up with sin and go into self-destruct mode. He won't relent until He rescues you! *It's because He loves you!* He doesn't want to see you destroyed and He doesn't want that thing *influencing and affecting and destroying others through you!*

You can go and read Romans Chapter 5 and 6 and study there about the grace of God. *But one thing you that will begin to see and discover is that* **grace is not there <u>as an overdraft-facility</u> so that you can continue in sin and just ask God to forgive you again and again while you just continue to deliberately walk blindfolded even though all the lights are already turned on in the house!**

<u>An overdraft-facility</u> in a bank account is more or less the same as a credit card. When this

little overdraft-provision is attached to your account it means:

'I don't have enough money to write a check for this or that, but it's all right. At least I have an overdraft-facility, at least I can spend more than my bank account actually has and not worry about it. The bank will cover me and tolerate my little transgression and put up with my over-spending. I'll just make up for it later with interest to satisfy the bank.'

Listen, the grace of God was meant to deliver you from that sin and its influence.

The grace of God was given to you so that you can come into *the <u>rule</u> of righteousness, so that righteousness might bring you <u>into dominion</u> over sin, and every opportunity to sin!*

1 Corinthians 15:34,

"***<u>Awake to righteousness</u>, and sin not.***"

Listen, we need to <u>awake</u> to righteousness *and appreciate it and treasure it and indulge in its fullness, its abundance, its beauty and glory and deliciousness.*

And then we will appropriate it and despise *and therefore dispel* sin from our lives! Sin will lose *its attraction and appeal!* That's the will of God the Father and Jesus. Amen!

The Holy Spirit who comes to dwell in us introduces to our spirits *righteousness.* In the light of the glory of *that righteousness,* He begins to expose to us sin for what it truly is, in all its ugliness. *He is the One who helps us overcome.*

You see, sin is nothing other than *alternative, short-sighted, and short-lived fulfillment.*

When you fall in love with Jesus and with your righteousness and with His Spirit and with Father God, then it is so easy *to fall out of love <u>with every other alternative</u>!*

Chapter 7

Righteousness: The Only Treasure Worth Pursuing

John 14:23,

"If <u>anyone</u> **loves Me, he will keep** (believe and embrace and value) **My word; and My Father will love him <u>and we will come to him and make our home with him.</u>**"

You see, there is the mansion, *the large glorious dwelling place.* **He comes to *live,* He comes to *dwell,* and He comes to *release in our spirits the liberty* of the sons of God.**

"The boundary lines have fallen for us in pleasant places; surely we have a delightful inheritance."

We are the very temple of the living God, the *dwelling place* of the Spirit of God. This intimate embrace and fellowship with God here *in our bosom* is truly, in all reality, the only treasure we have in these earthen vessels.

This is the only treasure worth pursuing.

Listen, there is no treasure *in the stature, in the glory* of the flesh. There really is no treasure *in the abilities and the talents or personality and identity* of the flesh. **But our only treasure is in the identity of our spirit-being! Our only treasure is being united again with our origin, our life-Source! Our only treasure is in the One who comes to <u>dwell</u> within us.**

It's the only treasure worth pursuing! It's the only treasure we have **of lasting value and influence** *upon our lives.*

It's also the only treasure worth sharing with this world. It's the only thing worth ministering to anyone: their true identity and the very presence and love of God.

Their inclusion, their righteousness restored to them and given to them as a gift in Christ, in the work of redemption, is the only thing worth ministering to this world.

Isaiah 40:6 & 7,

6 "**All flesh is grass, and all its loveliness is like the flower of the field**.

7 **The grass withers, the flower fades, <u>UNLESS</u>** the breath of the Lord blows upon it; <u>surely the people are grass</u>."

Paul himself also said, *"I place no confidence in the flesh ...whatever gain I had ...my education …my social standing …I count it as refuse* (dung).*"*

*"…**in comparison with the excellence of knowing Him.**"* - Philippians 3

I want you to read John chapter 14 again here in the next few pages. Read all the way through Chapter 15 and 16 until the end of Chapter 17 **in order to *get the full impact of the things I am saying. They are all connected and in the light of this teaching they will open up to you in a new way.***

John 14, 15, 16 and 17:

14:1 *"Let not your hearts be troubled;* **believe in God, believe also in Me***."*

2 *In My Father's house are many dwelling places,* (abiding places, rooms, abodes, mansions)*; if it were not so, I wouldn't have told you, '**I go to prepare a place <u>for you</u>**.'*

3 *And if* (since) *I go and **prepare a place for you**, I will come again, and receive you to Myself; that **where I am, <u>there</u> you may be also***.

4 *And you know the way where I am going.*

5 *Thomas said to Him, "Lord, we do not know where You are going, how do we know the way?*

6 *Jesus said to him, '**I am** the way, and the truth* (I am reality)*, and **the life*** (the abundant, eternal life; the fulfilled life; joy and contentment; love; a maximum life; the greatest life you can live; life in its essence) *No one comes to the Father* (can know God intimately or fellowship with Him)*, but through Me* (through My work of redemption I am about to accomplish)*.*

7 *If you had **known** Me, you would have **known** My Father also; **from now on you know Him, and have seen Him**.*

8 *Phillip said to Him, 'Lord, show us the Father, and it is enough for us.'*

9 *Jesus said to him, 'Have I been so long with you, and yet you have not **come to know** Me, Phillip? **He who has seen Me has seen the Father.** How do you say, 'Show us the Father?''*

10 *Do you not BELIEVE that **I am in the Father, and the Father is in Me**?*

*The words that I say to you I do not speak on My own initiative, **but the Father abiding in Me does His works**.*

11 *Believe Me that **I am in the Father, and the Father in Me;** otherwise believe on account of the works themselves.*

12 *Truly, truly,* **(I'm stating a fact and I'm trying to fully persuade you when)**, *I say to you, he who believes in Me, the works that I do shall he do also; and greater works than these shall he do;* <u>*because I go to the Father*</u>*.*

13 *And whatever you ask in My name,* <u>*that will I do*</u>*,* **that the Father may be glorified in the Son***.*

14 *If you ask anything in My name, I will do it.*

15 *If you love Me, keep* (believe and value, treasure, cherish) *My commandments* (my sayings, the things I strongly want you to believe).

16 *And I will ask the Father, and He will give you another Helper,* **that He may be with you** **(**<u>abide</u> **with you)** <u>***forever***</u>*,*

17 **that is the Spirit of Truth***, whom the world cannot receive, because it neither* **sees** *Him nor* **knows** *Him; but* <u>**you know Him**</u>**,** *for He dwells with you* **(in Me)***, and WILL BE* <u>***IN YOU***</u>*.*

18 *I will not leave you orphans; I will come to you"*

(by way of My resurrected Spirit, that Spirit of Truth and glory coming to indwell you; establishing your faith, establishing the truth in your hearts, establishing and cementing our relationship, establishing your conviction and your persuasion in these things, cementing you in intimacy with Me, and thereby also enabling you, and anointing you with power for ministry to others.)

19 *"After a little while the world will **see** Me no more; **but you will <u>see</u> Me** (behold Me); Because I live **you will <u>live</u>** also.*

20 *At that day **you shall KNOW <u>that I am in My Father, and you in Me, and I in you</u>**.*

21 *He who has My commandments* (my sayings, the things I told you so strongly to believe) *and keeps* (believes and values, treasures, cherishes) *them, it is he who loves Me; And **he who loves Me shall be loved by My Father, and I will love him and reveal** (will disclose; make known) *Myself* **(in full; in reality)** *to him.*

22 *Judas* (not Iscariot) *said to Him, 'Lord, how is it that You **will manifest** (are going to disclose, make real) **Yourself to us**, and not to the world?'*

23 *Jesus answered and said to him, 'If <u>anyone</u> **loves Me,** he will keep* (believe and value, treasure and cherish) *My word; and **My Father will love him, and We will come to him, and make Our home** (abode) **with him.**'*

24 *He who does not love Me does not keep* (believe and value) *My words; and **the word***

which you hear is not Mine, but the Father's who sent Me*.*

25 *These things I have spoken to you while being present,* ***abiding with you****.*

26 *But the Helper, the Holy Spirit, whom the Father will send in My name, He will teach you all things* (that I have done for you)*, and bring to your remembrance all things that I said to you* (concerning truth; concerning the work of redemption; concerning this place I am about to go and prepare for you)*.*

27 *Peace I leave with you,* ***My peace I give to you;*** *not as the world gives, do I give to you. Let not your heart be troubled, nor let it be* (fearful) *afraid.*

28 *You have heard Me say to you, 'I am going away, and* (then) *I will come* (back) *to you.'*

If you loved Me, you would rejoice ***because I am going to the Father*** (My Father and your Father)*;' for the Father is greater than I."*

(He is the One making all this happen, making it all a reality. And all this has everything to do with you, it is all for your benefit.)

29 *"And now I have told you before it comes to pass, that* <u>*when it does come to pass*</u>*,* ***you may believe****.*

30 *I will no longer talk much with you, for the ruler of this world is coming, and **he has nothing in Me**.*

31 *But that **the** (whole) **world may know** that I love the Father, and **as the Father gave Me commandment, even so I do**. Arise, let us go from here."*

15:1 *"I am the true vine* (the true source of your pleasure and enjoyment, of your life and of your fruit), *and My Father is the vine dresser.*

2 *Every branch in Me that does not bear fruit* (every dead, religious, lifeless, idea or conduct in your life not inspired and given life to in Me), *He takes away; and every branch that bears fruit He prunes it* (every truth He clarifies; every deception and inaccurate thought that wastes energy and robs your life He severs and removes from you), *that it* (the truth you know and enjoy nourishment from) *may bear more fruit.*

3 *You are already set apart* (clean, brought into My greater life) *because of the word* (the truth) *which I have spoken to you.*

4 **<u>Abide in Me, and I in you</u>. As the branch cannot bear fruit of itself, unless it abides in the vine, so neither can you, unless you abide in Me.**

5 *I am the vine, you are the branches* (you come out of Me, I am your source, you are the

product of the truth; the revelation; the life I have put in you)*;*

He who abides in Me, and I in him, he bears much fruit*; for without Me* **(apart from Me; My Spirit-influence of eternal truth)** *you can do nothing.*

6 *If anyone does not abide in Me, he is cast out as a branch;"*

(**he excludes himself** through stubborn unbelief and stubborn persistence, in lies and deception, the things of darkness)

"…and is withered (dries up, becomes empty, void of life)*; and they gather them, and throw them into the fire, and they are burned.*

(He is not referring to people here, being gathered up and thrown into the fire, and burned, He is merely referring to what we do with withered branches that fall off the vine. But if you want to read more into it, then consider the fact that people are usually consumed by the fire of their own destructive passions.)

7 *If you* **abide** *in Me, and My words* **abide** *in you, ask whatever you desire, and it shall be done for you.*

8 *By this My Father is glorified, that you bear much fruit* (it's the word bearing fruit through you)*; and so you are My disciples.*

9 ***Just as the Father has loved Me, I have also loved you; ABIDE IN MY LOVE*** **(We know and have believed the love God has for us)**.

10 ***If you keep My commandments*** **(believe and value and treasure My sayings; the things I told you so strongly and clearly to believe)**, ***you will abide in My love, just as I have kept My Father's commandments, and abide in His love***.

11 *These things I have spoken to you,* ***that My joy may*** **(be in you and)** ***remain in you, and that your joy may be*** <u>***made full***</u>.

12 *This is My commandment, that you love one another* ***just as I have loved you***"

(because I have loved you, you are set free and filled up with love to now love one another; actually it is Father God's truth and indwelling that is the inspiration of that love.)

13 *Greater love has no one than this, than to lay down one's life for his friends.*

14 *You are My friends if you do* (believe and come under the influence of) *whatever I command you* (to believe and treasure).

15 *No longer do I call you servants, for a servant does not know what his master is doing; but I have called you friends,* ***for all things that I have heard from My Father***

(concerning eternal truth, and about what I am about to accomplish, and about this place in the bosom of the Father that I am preparing for you) *I have made known to you*.

16 *You did not choose Me, but I chose you and appointed you, that you should go and bear fruit, and that your fruit should remain, that whatever you ask the Father in My name, He may give you.*

17 *This I command you: that you love one another"*

(There is no other conclusion to redemption; no other outcome to God's indwelling.)

18 *"If the world hates you, you know that it hated Me before it hated you.*

19 **If you were of the world,** *the world would love its own;* **but because you are not of this world,** *but I chose you out of the world, therefore the world hates you.*

20 *Remember the word that I said to you, 'A servant is not greater than his master.' If they persecuted Me, they will also persecute you.* **If they kept My word, they will keep yours also***.*

21 *But all these things they will do to you for My name's sake,* **because they do not know <u>Him</u> who sent Me***"*

(Even though some of them think they do, but they have come to the wrong conclusion about God and about the gospel; they worship a distorted picture of God they received through religion, a god of their own making.)

22 *"If I had not come and spoken to them, they would have no sin, but **now they have no excuse** for their sin."*

(Their sin is their stubborn persistence in unbelief, clinging to wrong religious ideas based on lies and deception, inherited through their forefathers who were blind also.)

23 *He who hates Me hates My Father also.*

24 *If I had not done among them the works which no one else did, they would have no sin; but now they have **seen*** (and yet have refused to believe) *and also hated both Me and My Father.*

25 *But this happened that the word might be fulfilled which is written in their law,*

'They hated Me without a cause.'

26 *But when the Helper comes, **whom I shall send to you** from the Father, **the Spirit of Truth, who proceeds from the Father,** He will testify of Me.*

27 *And you also will bear witness, because you have been with Me from the beginning."*

16:1 *"These things I have spoken to you, that you should not be made to stumble*

2 They will put you out of the synagogues; yes, the time is coming that whoever kills you will think that he offers God service.

*3 And these things they will do to you **because they have not known the Father nor Me**.*

4 But these things I have told you that when the time comes, you may remember that I told you of them. And these things I did not say to you at the beginning, because I was with you.

5 But now I go away to Him who sent Me, and none of you asks Me, (in other words: stop insulting My goodness and hurting my feelings by asking Me) *'Where are you going?'"*

(as if I intend to ever abandon you)

6 "But because I have said these things to you, sorrow has filled your hearts.

*7 Nevertheless I tell you the truth. **It is to your advantage that I go away;** for if I do not go away, **the Helper will** not **come to you**; but if I depart, **I will send Him to you**.*

*8 And when He has come, He will convict **the (whole) world** of sin, **and of righteousness**, and of judgment:*

(not our judgment or the judgment to come, but **the judgment of our enemy**)

9 *of sin, because they do not believe in Me*

(their sin is their unbelief; their refusal to believe; they are without excuse. In the light of truth and faith that gets revealed to a person by the Holy Spirit, unbelief is exposed for what it is: missing the mark, and it is therefore inexcusable, because it is at the heart of self-destruct mode and leads to death)*;*

10 *of righteousness,*

(the whole world is now made righteous in the work of redemption I am about to accomplish on mankind's behalf and the Holy Spirit comes to convict the world of that reality)

*...***because I go to My Father** *and you see Me no more;*

11 *of judgment,* **because (in the death of Jesus, in the work of redemption)** *the ruler of this world is judged* **(He is defeated and made powerless)***."*

(I want you to notice that **the Spirit of Truth's focus is on conviction of <u>*truth,*</u> conviction of righteousness, and conviction of the enemy's defeat, <u>not on conviction of sin</u>.**

The Holy Spirit is not called **The Spirit of <u>Truth</u>** *for nothing.* **Since sin is but <u>the fruit</u>**

of deception, the work of redemption and its Truth <u>is the antidote</u> to sin. It's the conviction of <u>this</u> Truth that frees us from sin.

Stubborn persistence in unbelief and deception is a refusal to be persuaded in the truth of redemption and of course there is greater condemnation upon those who do this, there is a greater struggle in their hearts with fear, and a condemning accusing voice, because in the light of redemption truth there is no more valid excuse for their stubbornness and for their persistence in an empty life of sin.

There is no escape of sin and condemnation and the experience of its consequences <u>outside of that truth of redemption</u>.

They judge themselves unworthy of eternal life and that in and of itself is their judgment because the Father judges no one and neither did the Son come into the world to condemn the world but that the world through Him might be saved.

Stubborn persistence in unbelief and deception; that self-deception, a refusal to be persuaded of truth is the only thing that gets in the Holy Spirit's way and must be dealt with. It must be removed if at all possible!

The only solution to that, the only way for the Holy Spirit to thoroughly deal with that and to remove it is **for the Spirit of Truth to clarify truth in order to thoroughly persuade the unpersuaded so that they too may be free!**

Outside of that clarifying and persuasion in Truth there is no salvation. There is no rescuing them and freeing them from self-destruct mode.*)*

16:12 *"I still have many things to say to you, but you cannot bear them now."*

(You won't genuinely comprehend them now in this wounded emotional state – I mean, who wants to hear that their best friend is about to die a gruesome death – and then in that confused horrified state, you are now supposed to believe that He is coming back *but in a different form* and that **somehow things will be the same as they were before** – that is hard for anyone to swallow.)

13 *"However,* **when He, the Spirit of Truth, has come, He will guide you into all truth;** *for He will not speak on His own authority, but whatever He hears He will speak;*

…and He will tell you things to come."

(The subsequent glories that follow the cross; the salvation that is about to be ours, the righteousness that is about to be restored *are*

the future things He will speak of and reveal in full.**)**

You see, those things were yet to come then, **but they have now already fully come and that is what the Spirit of Truth was sent to come and make known and establish.**

Of course, what I am sharing is not to try and undo the reality of the Holy Spirit *sometimes telling us and showing us things to come, even warning us for our protection sometimes through a "word of knowledge" or a vision or a prophetic word. After all, He cares about the every-day, nitty-gritty details of our lives.*

But even if He didn't show you something before it happened, **don't start questioning His nearness or your closeness with Him, just trust Him! He is still there, He is still the I AM, the ever living, very present One, ready to guide you and help you through whatever you may face in life!**

'My sheep hear My voice!'

This is what the Spirit of Truth will come to do, not get you preoccupied with supposed future, vague prophetic events.

No,

14 "...He will glorify **Me**, for **He will take of what is Mine (My righteousness made available to you)** *and declare it to you.*

15 **All things that the Father has are Mine** (to enjoy). **Therefore I said that He will take of what is Mine and declare it to you** (for you to now enjoy as well).

16 **A little while, and you will not see Me** (in the flesh)**; and again a little while, and you will see Me** (by revelation knowledge, by insight and understanding into truth, by grasping Spirit REALITY), *because I go to the Father.*

17 *Then some of His disciples said among themselves, "What is this that He says to us, 'A little while, and you will not see Me; and again a little while, and you will see Me'; and, 'because I go to the Father'?"*

18 *They said therefore, "What is this that He says, 'A little while'? We do not know what He is saying."*

19 *Now Jesus knew that they desired to ask Him, and he said to them, "Are you inquiring among yourselves about what I said,* '**A little while, and you will not see Me; and again a little while, and you will see Me?**'

20 *Most assuredly, I say to you that you will weep and lament, but the world* (in their ignorance) *will rejoice* (at my crucifixion)*; and you will be sorrowful,* **but your sorrow will be turned into joy**.

21 *A woman, when she is in labor, has sorrow because her hour has come; but* **as soon as she has given birth** *to a child, she* **no longer remembers the anguish, for joy** *that a human being has been born into the world.*

22 *Therefore you now have sorrow;* **but I will see you again (I will be raised from the dead, and I will come again to you in Spirit form)** *and your heart will rejoice, and your joy no one will take from you.*

23 *And in that day you will ask Me nothing* (anymore because you will now be directly linked to the Father, to My Father, and YOUR Father). *Most assuredly, I say to you, whatever you ask the Father in My name He will give you.*

24 *Until now you have asked nothing in My name. Ask, and you will receive, that your joy may be full.*

25 *These things I have spoken to you in figurative language* (like about the vine and the branches)*; but* **the time is coming (after my death and resurrection) when I will no longer speak to you in figurative language, but I will tell you plainly about the Father**."

(Hallelujah, we are living in that time NOW, where the Holy Spirit is unveiling to us everything, yes, even the deep things of the heart of God. He has come to lead us into all TRUTH!)

26 *In that day you will ask in My name, and **I do not say to you that I shall ask the Father for you**;*

27 ***for the Father Himself loves you, because you have loved Me, and have believed that I came from God.***

28 ***I came forth from the Father** and have come into the world. Again, I leave the world and go to the Father.*

29 *His disciples said to Him, 'See now You are speaking plainly, and using no figure of speech!*

30 *Now we are sure that You know all things, and have no need that anyone should question You. By this we believe that You came forth from God.'*

31 *Jesus answered them, 'Do you now believe?'*

32 *Indeed the hour is coming, yes, **has now come**, that you will be scattered, each to his own, and will leave Me alone. And yet I am not alone, **because the Father is with Me**.*

33 ***These things I have spoken to you, that in Me you may have peace**.*

*In the world you will have tribulation; but be of good cheer, **I have overcome the world**.*

17:1 *"Jesus spoke these words, lifted up His eyes to heaven, and said: Father, **the hour has come**. Glorify Your Son, that Your Son also may glorify You,*

2 *as **You have given Him authority over all flesh, that He should give eternal life to as many as You have given Him**.*

3 **<u>And this is eternal life, that they may know</u> (intimately know, fully know) <u>You, the only true God, and Jesus Christ whom You have sent</u>**.

4 *I have <u>glorified You</u> on the earth. I have <u>finished the work</u> **which You have given Me to do**."*

(He was already looking past the cross to the subsequent glories! For the joy set before Him, the joy of seeing us included, liberated, and restored, He endured the cross!)

5 *"And now, O Father, **glorify Me together with Yourself, with the glory which I had with You before the world was**."*

(His faith was so beautiful! He prayed so victoriously, with such confidence, such trust towards His Father, such finality of resolve, as if the cross was a minor thing lying ahead of Him. His faith saw past even the greatest trial of His life and was anchored beyond the cross in the living hope of an unhindered, uninterrupted future. He had such a grip on

ETERNAL REALITY, on His true identity, that it totally liberated Him from the temporal!)

6 *"**I have manifested Your name** (Your reputation as Father, Your love, Your person, Your very image and likeness) to the men whom You have given Me out of the world.*

***They were Yours*"** **(from the beginning – You formed them and fashioned them in their mother's womb, and gave them life, and clothed them with flesh. You are indeed their origin.)**

You gave them to Me (as intimate friends and disciples)*, and they have kept* (believed, valued and treasured) *Your word.*

7 *Now they have known that all things which You have given Me **are from You**.*

8 *For I have given them the words which You have given Me; and they have **received** (**welcomed, believed**) them, and have known surely that **I came forth from You;** and they have **believed** that **You sent Me**.*

9 *I pray for them. I do not pray for the world* (right now at this junction of time; they, My disciples, will do plenty of that later, after My departure,) *but* (right now, because they genuinely need it, I pray) *for those whom You have given Me, for **they are Yours**"*

(I leave them in Your capable hands, and I ask that You keep influencing them, reminding them of the truths they heard in the things I said. Protect them in that way from Satan's influence; especially now that I am going to be focused on and busy with the work of redemption, and won't be there for them for a short while.)

10 *"And* **all Mine are Yours, and Yours are Mine, and I am glorified in them***.*

11 *Now I am no longer in the world* (My resolve is set, the work is as good as done), *but these are in the world, and I come to You. Holy Father,* **keep** *through Your* **name** (through Your reputation as Father, and as lover of their souls) **those whom You have given Me, <u>that they may be one</u> (with Us and one another, just)** <u>as We are</u>*.*

12 *While I was with them in the world, I kept them in Your name. Those whom You gave Me I have kept and none of them are lost; except the son of perdition, just as the Scriptures have foretold.*

13 *But now I come to You, and* **these things I speak in the world, that they may have My joy fulfilled in themselves.**

14 *I have given them Your word;"*

(That truth I shared with them separated them from worldly thinking. They no longer think the way the world thinks, they are not under the same deception anymore.)

*"…and the world has hated them because **they are not of this world, just as I am not of this world**.*

15 I do not pray that You should take them out of the world, but that You should keep them from the evil one"

(From his influence; from a confused, deceived mind and an evil heart of unbelief)

*16 "**They are not of the world, <u>just as I am not of the world</u>**.*

*17 Set them apart **<u>by Your truth</u>*** (By Your reality). *Your word **is truth*** (Your word is reality)*.*

*18 **As You sent Me into the world, <u>I also send them into the world</u>**.*

*19 And for their sakes I set Myself apart, **that they also may be set apart** (sanctified, made clean, come into a love-commitment and develop a pure devotion to You) **by the truth**"*

(Which they not only heard from Me but saw in Me, in My very life, and love, and being.)

20 *"I do not pray for these alone,* ***but also for those who will believe in Me through their word****;*

21 ***that they all may be one****, as You Father, are in Me, and I in You;* ***that they also may be one in Us****, that the world* ***may believe*** *that You sent Me.*

22 ***And the glory*** *(*DOXA – the opinion, the truth that beautifies Me, the truth about our common identity and origin and righteousness, both Mine and theirs; even the Spirit of Truth; the very glory of God Himself) **which You gave Me** (that makes me attractive and full of love and anointing and full of power) **I have given them, that they may be one just as We are one***:*

23 ***I in them, and You in Me****; that they may be made perfect in one,* and that the world may know that ***You have sent me, and*** ***have loved them as You have loved Me****.*

24 ***Father, I desire that they also whom You gave Me*** ***may be with me where I am****, that they may behold My glory*** (My righteousness, My love, My authority and power, My very eternal person, My place of abiding in You, in Your love and Your power and Your eternal glory. I share Your executive authority. I desire that they may behold and share this glory) ***which You have given Me;***

for You loved Me before the foundation of the world*.*

25 *O righteous Father! The world has not known You,* ***but I have known You;*** *and these have known that You sent Me.*

26 ***And I have declared to them*** (the truth concerning You, Your love for them, and our common origin in You, both Mine and theirs,) ***<u>that the love with which You loved Me may be in them, and I in them</u>****."*

In the light of this teaching and by what is being said in these Scriptures, *a new door of opportunity is opened up to you today.* **You too may freely enter that place Jesus prepared for you.**

Chapter 8

For With the Heart One Believes

If, after reading this book, you now realize that Father God has indeed *restored YOUR original righteousness to you* and prepared a wonderful place *for YOU* of intimate friendship and enjoyment of fellowship and companionship with Him through Jesus' successful work of redemption, but you do not know how to enter into, or begin to live in, these realities and become fully joined to the Lord, to where sin and its influence are obliterated in your life, and times of refreshing may come to your life from the very presence of the Lord, the Scriptures tell us what is essential.

The Bible says in Romans 10:9-13,

9 *"...if you confess* (**HOMOLOGAO**) *with your mouth* (**say the same thing; come into agreement with God**: with His thoughts; with His truth; with what He did for you in the work of redemption and through) *the Lord Jesus;*

…and (therefore, **actually**) ***believe in your heart*** *that God has* (indeed) *raised Him from the dead"*

(Because the work was complete and now you can enjoy righteousness, deliverance, and salvation *if you believe these things and **truly come into agreement with God; it will become your reality, it will be yours to enjoy***)

*"...**you will be saved** (rescued, made whole; made complete).*

10 ***For with the heart one believes*** **(one's way into the enjoyment of)** *righteousness, and with the mouth <u>confession</u> is made;"*

(*"Confession"* **or HOMOLOGAO – to say the same thing; to be on the same page; to echo your agreement with God; to come into complete agreement; that full and total agreement is made** *because you are persuaded in your heart.***)**

*"...**resulting in salvation.***

11 *For the Scripture says, "**Whoever** believes in Him* (Jesus and His work of redemption) *will not be put to shame.*

13 ***For whoever*** **(anyone, everyone who)** ***calls upon the name of the Lord*** **(who identifies himself with the Lord, and the work of redemption, and discovers his place of belonging in God)** ***shall be saved**."*

For many it is not even necessary to pray some *"sinner's prayer"*. **They are already persuaded in their hearts and minds** *and*

simply begin to enjoy fellowship with Jesus and with their Maker, their Daddy, Father God. *But for some it starts with a simple prayer in and from their hearts.* After all He is there already, *the ever-living, present Spirit, the great I AM.*

If you feel you need to and choose to pray this prayer **because it echoes what is in your own heart,** be assured that God your Father hears every word *because He is not far from any one of us.* After all, we are His offspring, *and in Him we live and move and have our being.* He gives to all men life, breath, *and all other things. He hears your heart's cry and is ready to answer your prayer!*

Feel free to pray this now:

Father God, thank you that in Christ Jesus You forgave my trespasses and that You are not holding my ignorance against me.

Thank you for blotting out my sin on the cross and restoring me to righteousness!

Thank you for loving me and embracing me and accepting me back into Your bosom.

Jesus, thank you that I can share the beauty of your life and love with you!

Come and make your abode within me!

Come and live life with me, and come let us glorify the Father *and put His life on display in this one body!*

Let us exhibit *His love for people* together!

Thank you for opening my eyes!

Thank you for rescuing me out of ignorance and darkness!

Thank you for rescuing me out of self-destruct mode!

You have won my heart!

I love you!

Things between you and your Daddy God never need to be the same as they used to be. He desires **no distance, no separation.** He desires **closeness with you! He has already fully embraced you** and He stands ready to take you into that place **of intimate fellowship** Jesus prepared for YOU!

You no longer *need* sin in your life. *Its emptiness has robbed you long enough, its rule and dependency have been broken* and He will help you *defeat it totally in your life, no matter what kind of addiction you may be suffering from.*

His fullness, His joy, His love, His life, is now your portion!

You probably already feel different ...but, hey, don't depend on feelings! *This thing called TRUTH is so much bigger than your feelings.*

The Scripture says in 1 Corinthians 6:17 that,

*"He who is joined to the Lord **is one spirit with Him**"*

It also says in 2 Corinthians 5:17 that,

*"In Him you are a new creation, the old things have passed away, **behold all things have become new**."*

If you want to find out what it means to be that new creation, *you will find your answer in the New Testament portion of the Holy Bible.* In fact, if you want to grow in your relationship with God, the Word of God, Jesus, and the Word of redemption, testified to in the Scriptures, *must find it's rightful place of lordship in your heart.*

In 2 Peter 2:2 & 3, Peter encourages us to become just like newborn infants who desire their mother's milk. By saying this he basically means that **your very life depends upon your desire to keep feasting on the Word of Truth, the Gospel of your salvation, so that you may mature in your understanding of these things and grow up into the fullness of it.**

He puts it in such a way as to say that **your pursuit of resources that contain this message would almost be automatic, like an addiction,** *"…if indeed you have tasted that the Lord is good."*

Because your heart can't get enough, you may get bored with the knowledge of 1 + 1 = 2, but you cannot get bored with the knowledge of love!

The language of love is not boring. The love of God is not boring, especially now that it speaks personally to you and you know it intimately and your inner-being, your spirit, now knows it needs to keep feeding and feasting on these truths because it is God's intimate love-language to you!

In closing, I urge you to get yourself a copy of *"The Mirror Bible"* available online at: www.Amazon.com and several other book sellers.

If you want me or someone that is a part of our team to come and speak somewhere, or come and teach you and some of your friends about the gospel message and these redemption realities, simply contact us at www.LivingWordIntl.com. Or you can always find me on Facebook.

I pray that our Daddy, Father God Himself, who has richly given us all things to enjoy, may abundantly bless you with all the LIFE, LOVE and JOY you can handle, and that you would truly prosper in life and in health even as your soul prospers in this new place of righteousness and intimate friendship and fellowship and wholeness and right-being God has prepared *for US and for YOU!*

If your life has changed as a result of reading this book, *please get in touch with me and let me know.*

I would love to share your joy, *so that my joy in writing this book may be full!*

That which was from the beginning,

*which we have heard
(with our spiritual ears),
which we have seen
(with our spiritual eyes),
which we have looked upon
(beheld, focused our attention upon),
and which our hands have also handled
(which we have also experienced),*

concerning the Word of life,

we declare to you,

that you also may have this fellowship with us;

*and truly our fellowship is with the Father
and with His Son Jesus Christ.*

And these things we write to you that your joy may be full.

- 1 John 1:1-4

About the Author

Rudi & Carmen Louw together oversee and pastor a church: Living Word International. They also travel and minister both locally and internationally.

Rudi was born and raised in the country of South Africa, while Carmen grew up in Cortland, New York. They function in the ministry of reconciliation (2 Corinthians 5:18-21) and flow strongly in the gifts of the Holy Spirit and His anointing to teach, preach, prophesy, heal *and whatever is needed to touch peoples lives with the reality of God's love and power.*

God has given them keen insight into what He has to say to mankind in the work of redemption, concerning the revelation of and restoration of humanity's true identity. And therefore they emphasize THE GOSPEL; IN CHRIST REALITIES, the GRACE of God, the WORD OF RIGHTEOUSNESS and all such eternal truths essential to salvation and living of the CHRIST-LIFE.

They have been granted this wisdom and revelation into the knowledge of God by the resurrected Spirit of Jesus Christ, *to establish and strengthen believers in the faith of God, and to activate them in ministering to others.*

Not only are people set free from the poison and bondage of sin, condemnation and all kinds of intimidation, (upheld, strengthened and reinforced by age old religious ideas born out of ignorance and deception,) *but many are brought into a closer more intimate relationship with Father God as Daddy, through the accurate teaching and unveiling of the gospel message, prophetic words, healings and miracles.*

Rudi & Carmen are closely knitted together in friendship with several other effective Christians, church fellowships, and groups of believers who share the same revelation and passion.

www.ingramcontent.com/pod-product-compliance
Lightning Source LLC
Chambersburg PA
CBHW071122090426
42736CB00012B/1981